## PRAISE FOR PATRICK CROUGH

Patrick Crough has provided an illuminating and insightful look into the work of a major case crimes investigator. By selecting these cases for review, Patrick has shown the depth of knowledge and skill necessary to today's investigator. He has accurately portrayed what it takes to solve a major crime, both from a trained and skilled investigative perspective and from an inner psychological mind-set. He combines police procedure with personal insights in an informative, easy-to-read and entertaining manner. This book should be a "must read" for any police officer, investigator or anyone interested in police procedural issues.

— Dr. Wayman C. Mullins
professor of criminal justice, Texas State University

CHRONICLES OF A
# ROCHESTER
## Major Crimes Detective

Confronting Evil &
Pursuing Truth

*Patrick Crough*

Charleston · London

THE
History
PRESS

Published by The History Press
Charleston, SC 29403
www.historypress.net

Copyright © 2011 by Patrick Crough
All rights reserved

First published 2011

Manufactured in the United States

ISBN 978.1.60949.377.6


Library of Congress Cataloging-in-Publication Data

Crough, Patrick.
Chronicles of a Rochester major crimes detective : confronting evil and
pursuing truth / Patrick Crough.
p. cm.
ISBN 978-1-60949-377-6
1. Criminal investigation--New York (State)--Rochester. 2. Criminal
investigation--New York (State)--Rochester--Case studies. 3. Murder--New
York (State)--Rochester--Case studies. I. Title.
HV6534.R624C76 2011
364.152'30974789--dc23
2011035032

*This book is dedicated to the victims whose tragic stories
are shared in the following pages.*

*Vince Romano, my brother in Christ, now in glory: your words of encouragement
and loving support will never be forgotten.*

# Contents

Preface                                             9

Case 1: St. Valentine's Day Murders                11
Case 2: Hate + Revenge = Murder                    67
Case 3: Spawn of Satan                             93
Case 4: Murder in Pittsford                       113

Final Comments                                    137
About the Author                                  139

# Preface

*The authorities are God's servants, sent for your good. But if you are doing wrong, of course you should be afraid, for they have the power to punish you. They are God's servants, sent for the very purpose of punishing those, who do what is wrong.*
*—Romans 13:4 (NLT)*

Confronting evil in the pursuit of truth defines the life of a Major Crimes–Special Victims Police investigator. I spent twenty years doing so as an investigator and investigator-sergeant in the Major Crimes Unit of the Monroe County Sheriff's Office in Rochester, New York, the majority of my twenty-seven-year career in law enforcement. We investigated homicides and suspicious deaths, violent assaults that resulted in serious physical injury, sexual assaults, crimes against children, robberies, police-involved shootings, and confidential special investigations at the direction of the sheriff of Monroe County.

You might be asking, why did I write this book? Well, I have several reasons. First, I believe that some of the cases I worked as a Major Crimes investigator are worth sharing for the purpose of edifying others about the inner workings of a major criminal investigation. Sharing one's personal and professional experiences with the generations that follow is an important component of learning in any field. This is especially true in the world of Major Crimes police detectives. Being exposed to various crime scenes and situations vicariously through the experiences of seasoned colleagues is invaluable to the development of a criminal investigator.

I know that throughout my own career I often sought out certain police investigators who came before me. These were individuals who had proven themselves, one investigation after another, to be successful and dedicated to their calling: solving serious crimes and putting together prosecutable cases. This leads to my second reason for writing this book: it is my tribute to them for their willingness to share their knowledge and experience with a fledgling police officer and detective and my attempt to pay it forward to those who now follow in the never-ending fight against evil in the pursuit of truth.

I also must admit that I have chosen to write about some of my more memorable experiences to leave what I think is a critical legacy to my younger brethren. This legacy is twofold. I hope that from these recollections they will recognize the necessity of always pursuing truth, even when confronted with the most evil among us, in a lawful manner. I also want them to leave their ego at home and to strive to be remembered as a trusted and competent police investigator by those with whom they work. There is no better compliment to a cop than the genuine respect of colleagues who worked with him or her, day in and day out.

While every Major Crimes investigation I worked was important, the ones featured in the following pages are some of the cases that stand out in my mind. The content of each of these investigations is real and based on factual information. I changed the names of some of the people (including some suspects) to protect the identities of the innocent. An asterisk will be located next to a name when it first appears in the book to signify that it has been changed.

Also, for the purpose of clarification, the terms "detective" and "investigator" should be considered one and the same. Police departments throughout our nation use both titles for those sworn members who investigate the more serious crimes committed in their jurisdictions.

It is my sincere hope that these experiences will benefit and inspire those individuals who desire or are commencing a career in law enforcement to do their best every day regardless of the job. Serving as a law enforcement officer in the United States is both an honor and a privilege; we are chosen and trained to serve and protect the most valuable asset this country has: its people. We must never lose sight of this mission and the law that helps us identify and rid true threats to it.

# St. Valentine's Day Murders

*I have been driven many times to my knees by overwhelming conviction
that I had nowhere else to go. My wisdom, and that of all about me,
seemed insufficient for the day.*
—*Abraham Lincoln*

## SATURDAY, FEBRUARY 14, 2009, 5:45 A.M.

The pager's all-too-familiar, annoying beep jolted me awake in the
early morning darkness. This is not healthy, I thought to myself as I
struggled to get out of bed and grab it from the dresser six feet away.
I had deliberately kept the pager that far from my bed to prevent me
from just reaching over to my nightstand to turn it off. If my feet weren't
forced to hit the floor, I knew that I might easily slip back into a slumber
and not answer the page.

The cold night air in the bedroom only exasperated my misery. Nearly
twenty years of being awakened out of a deep sleep sucked. We in the field
call it "blood money." The overtime is great, but I have no doubt it has
taken years off my life. I stepped out of the bedroom to answer the page so
as not to disturb Suzanne, my wife of twenty-nine years, who had grown
accustomed to the middle-of-the-night call outs. After stumbling like a
drunk to the kitchen table and dropping onto one of the chairs, I called my
supervisor, Sergeant Doug Comanzo.

"What's up, Doug?" I asked miserably.

"Morning, Patrick," Sergeant Comanzo responded in his usual empathetic, monotone voice. "Sorry to wake you, but we've got two shot dead in the parking lot of Lakeside hospital and a third on the way to Strong in critical condition." Strong Memorial Hospital, a part of the University of Rochester Medical School, served as the only certified medical trauma center for a ten-county region in western New York.

"Anyone in custody?" I asked while supporting my forehead in my left hand and cradling the phone against my right ear with the other. I kept my eyes closed.

"No," he responded. "At this time we don't know who the shooter is."

"Alright. I'm about forty-five minutes to an hour out," I said.

"Thank you, Patrick. See you there," Sergeant Comanzo said with genuine appreciation in his voice.

Like so many other foggy-minded exchanges over the telephone during the late hours of a night or wee hours of a dark morning, there was minimal emotion on either end of a call-out notification. It was business as usual. Although, at times, Sergeant Comanzo would catch an attitude from one of his sleep-deprived detectives in the Major Crimes Unit, most of whom possessed several more years of investigative experience than him. But Sergeant Comanzo never faltered or wavered from his steady and easygoing style of managing the cast of odd characters he was assigned to supervise.

A former Division III college hockey player and scratch golfer, the dark-haired and spectacled forty-something Comanzo possessed an abundance of wisdom and excellent interpersonal skills that more than made up for his lack of experience in the area of major crime investigations. He got the most out of the stable of unruly and hotblooded thoroughbred investigators that made up the Monroe County Sheriff's Office Major Crimes Unit. Year in and year out, our unit's clearance rate was in the low to mid-nineties—a remarkable statistic in the world of major crimes and special victims investigations. Sergeant Comanzo's management style of empowering his people to do their jobs and holding them accountable to work their cases in a timely manner was a significant reason for such success.

"What is it?" my wife asked. Wearing her sweat suit pajamas, she was wrapped in her usual cocoon of warm blankets and pillows in our bed. I stumbled toward the master bath not wanting to stub my toes in the near total darkness of the room.

"Triple shooting, two dead at the scene, one nearly dead on the way to the hospital," I answered as I turned on the shower to let the water run hot. My tone was matter-of-fact.

"Dear God," she whispered. "Who?"

"No idea," I answered. "But I think our Saturday Valentine's Day dinner plans are off for tonight, baby. I'm sorry."

Suzanne did not respond. She has endured countless interruptions, postponements and cancellations over the past twenty years. Working as a Major Crimes investigator is not just a job or a career; it's a lifestyle. My wife and family have sacrificed much. I was an absentee dad and husband during my nearly two-decade-long tenure in the unit.

The bitter cold wind out of the northwest stung my face as I walked into the early-morning darkness. There was hardly any snow on the iron-hard frozen ground. The leftover moisture on my skin and hair from the hot shower immediately iced over during the short walk to my take-home, unmarked police vehicle. I scraped off the thick and stubborn coating of clouded ice on the windows in a hastened fashion since time was of the essence. Once Major Crimes is called, no one does anything at the scene until we arrive. The sooner we get there, the better.

Lakeside hospital was a small medical facility and nursing home in Brockport, New York, which is located in the northwest corner of Monroe County, a short distance from the south shore of the Great Lake of Ontario. I reside in the northeast corner of the county. It is a forty-five-minute drive when doing the speed limit in normal traffic. Low-level flying in my police cruiser along the deserted highways of the early morning got me to Lakeside in just under half an hour.

Once on scene, I parked in the staging area some distance from the actual crime scene and hooked up with Sergeant Comanzo. The sun was just peeking out, bringing on the dawn. He sat in the front passenger seat of my vehicle and shared what he had gleaned from the police personnel on scene thus far: one dead male and one dead female were lying in the hospital's deserted south-side parking lot about fifty yards ahead of us. The third victim was a female and still alive. She had driven herself to the Brockport Village Police Department station about one mile from the scene. All Sergeant Comanzo could tell me about the shooter was that he appeared to be a light-skinned black or Hispanic male who left the scene in an unknown vehicle.

Except for the village police officer and emergency medical services personnel who responded to the parking lot to check the condition of the victims, the scene remained untouched. Per our normal operating procedure, we were waiting on the crime scene technicians to set up and take the initial photographs of the crime scene before we entered it. According to Sergeant Comanzo, the Brockport Village Police chief was out of town on vacation but was seriously considering having his officers take over the investigation since the hospital parking lot was located just inside the village boundary.

Such a move would have been both ballsy and stupid. It would be unwise for an eight-man police department to act as the lead agency on this type of case. A small police department of that size did not possess the resources or manpower to carry a case of this scale. Apparently the chief thought better of it after a compromise was reached with our department's brass. We agreed to keep one of his officers directly involved in the investigation. I had no problem with this decision. I have always been a proponent of keeping the uniformed officers involved in major cases, for they benefit from the experience and exposure. I also never had a problem working alongside other departments toward the same goal: catching bad guys. The "worker bees" always find a way to get along and get the job done when the upper echelon of their departments avoid the customary "fiefdom" turf wars and stay out of the way.

Sergeant Comanzo assigned Investigator Steve Peglow and me to be the primary case agents. The primary case agents take ownership of the investigation and usually have the most influence regarding the strategic and investigative decisions of the case. This method has proven to be the most effective way to investigate major crimes and homicides. The rest of the unit acts as the support cast, taking investigative assignments from the primary investigators to move the case forward. The information and opinions generated by the support cast are valued, but ultimately the two case agents make the investigative decisions.

Alternative strategies are far less effective. For example, I find investigating major cases by committee is like watching five monkeys trying to have sex with a football at the same time. Everyone starts going in their own directions with the case and offering up unneeded opinions. This ultimately leads to polarization and dissension. And, inevitably, if no one owns the case then no one is going to care about the investigation when it goes cold.

I've seen major, high-profile cases investigated in this manner, and they rarely turn out successful. Someone has to be the voice of the case. They live and die with the investigation until it is either solved or deemed cold and tucked away in the file cabinet for a while.

After the initial crime scene photographs were taken, the investigative team exited our warm unmarked police vehicles into the frigid winter air and entered the parking lot for our first look. The crime scene encompassed a large portion of the empty parking area. I observed a deceased white male lying on his back along the south edge of the parking lot. He was identified as Randall Norman. A large pool of blood surrounded his head and part of his upper torso. He appeared to be in his late thirties to early forties. I then observed a deceased white female, who looked to be in her twenties, lying in a prone position with her arms at her sides. She had suffered an obvious gunshot wound to the back of her head, which was adjacent to a large pool of blood and brain tissue. The woman, who was employed at the hospital and working at the time of the shooting, was identified as Mary Silliman.

A late-model silver minivan was located approximately forty feet west of Ms. Silliman's body. The minivan, which was determined to belong to Ms. Silliman, was parked in a diagonal position with the front end pointing slightly southeast. The driver's door was wide open, and the motor was running. I observed a woman's purse on the vehicle's carpeted floor next to the driver's seat and a cell phone lying on the floor next to it. Small blood droplets were located near the corner of the lower sidewall of each tire. No other blood was visible on or around the vehicle.

Several shell casings from a .40-caliber semiautomatic pistol, a pair of female shoes and ear warmers that appeared to belong to Ms. Silliman were located in the middle area of the parking lot in between the two deceased victims and the silver minivan. We also found additional .40-caliber shell casings in the middle of the roadway that bordered the south side of the parking lot. An empty ammunition magazine from a semiautomatic pistol was observed on the ground next to the roadside curb several feet from the body of Randall Norman. I was advised by one of the crime scene technicians that the magazine appeared to be from a Glock semiautomatic pistol.

After examining the crime scene, I spoke with Investigators Andy White, Scott Walsh and Deputy Kevin McCory, who were conducting a canvass of the hospital employees inside the hospital. They learned that Ms. Silliman was having problems with her live-in boyfriend, *Jamal Winston, who was described to be violent and abusive toward her and suspected of using illegal drugs and possessing firearms. Ms. Silliman had advised other employees that Winston was jealous of all men she had contact with.

We also learned that Ms. Silliman may have had a personal relationship budding with her former night-shift supervisor, Frank Garcia, who reportedly had been propositioning Ms. Silliman for sex. Allegedly, on at least one occasion, Mr. Garcia offered Ms. Silliman hundreds of dollars to have sex with him. It was suspected that Jamal Winston might have learned of Mr. Garcia's propositions toward Ms. Silliman, causing Winston to become more physically abusive toward her.

Upon learning about the domestic violence and potential for it to carry over to the workplace, the hospital administrators set up a safety plan for Ms. Silliman and the rest of the night staff. A memo had been distributed and posted the night before the shooting, directing employees working the night shift to utilize the buddy system when exiting the hospital. Employees also were directed not to take their outdoor smoke breaks alone.

While speaking with one of the hospital supervisors, I learned that Frank Garcia had been terminated by Lakeside hospital recently due, in part, to his inappropriate behavior toward the female staff he supervised. He allegedly threatened to get even for what he viewed as an unjustified action on the part of the hospital administration. This threat was viewed to be in the form of a lawsuit. Garcia had never shown any signs of potential violence, according to hospital staff.

Still early morning and very cold, the investigative team decided to muster at the Brockport Diner for a quick warm breakfast and to formulate our investigative plan. The crime scene had been inspected and was now being processed by the crime scene technicians. The initial canvass of the hospital and surrounding houses had been completed. Nothing remarkable had been gained.

As was our custom, we preferred to discuss the case in private away from outside influence. Over eggs and coffee, we all agreed that Jamal Winston had to be located and interviewed as soon as possible. I also suggested that a team drive over to Frank Garcia's residence in Hamlin, a town located just northwest of Brockport, to confirm that he was still home in bed with his wife. As long as he had sleep in his eyes, we could quickly exclude him given that the shooting reportedly occurred around five in the morning.

It was easy to get tunnel vision and focus on the most obvious suspect. In this case that was Ms. Silliman's reportedly abusive live-in boyfriend, Jamal Winston. However, it was important that we kept an open mind and considered all possibilities. While speculation, hypothesizing and theorizing have their places in a criminal investigation, following the evidence and separating the pertinent information from the minutiae solve crimes.

Consequently, it takes a certain amount of experience to be successful at this process. Too many times I've seen detectives use the "shotgun method" simply to cover all the bases in order to satisfy the nervous and jerky types that oversee them. Although being known as a detective who turns over every stone may sound good to those who lack experience in major case investigations, the real object is to know what stones in the creek bed to disturb. If you are in the habit of turning over too many at once, you will just make the water murkier than it already is.

If nothing else, we thought Mr. Garcia, out of his wife's earshot, might be able to shed some light on the situation between Ms. Silliman and Jamal Winston. Garcia and Silliman reportedly shared smoke breaks outside during their shift. She may have confided in him. We learned he was her supervisor on the night shift. And then there was always the possibility they were engaged in a sexual relationship.

The description of the suspect and suspect vehicle was vague at best and nothing we could utilize as a workable lead. One thing we did know was that the suspect appeared to be either a light-skinned black or Hispanic male. That information had come from the victim who had survived the shooting and had driven herself to the police station while she nearly bled to death. She was identified as Audra Dillon.

Investigator Paul Siena was assigned to respond to the Emergency Trauma Center at Strong Memorial Hospital to interview Audra Dillon if she was still conscious. In his usual remarkable fashion, Investigator Siena was able to obtain the seriously injured woman's account before she went into surgery and relayed the information by telephone to Sergeant Comanzo, who was coordinating with the brass in the command post that had been set up at one of the firehouses near the crime scene. As a result, we learned the following: Ms. Dillon was driving Randall Norman to work early in the morning and proceeding past the south-side parking lot of the hospital when they observed a dark-skinned male beating a small blonde woman near the car parked in the lot. The male had the woman by the hair and was dragging her away from her vehicle. He punched and kicked her repeatedly.

Ms. Dillon stopped her 2001 maroon sedan. Both she and Mr. Norman stepped out and walked toward the parking lot from the south, all the while yelling at the man to stop hurting the woman or they were going to call 911. Mr. Norman made it to the parking lot in an attempt to intervene on behalf of Ms. Silliman amid the warnings from the suspect to stay out of it and leave. When Mr. Norman refused to back off, the suspect let go of the woman's hair, pulled out a handgun from his waist, crouched into a police shooting stance and fired at least three rounds at Mr. Norman.

Mr. Norman was struck in his chest, right arm and in the back of the head, behind his right ear, by the powerful .40-caliber rounds, causing his twisted and bullet-riddled body to drop to the pavement where he stood. The gunman then pivoted to his left, aimed at Ms. Silliman, who was running away with her back to him. He fired at least two rounds in her direction, striking Ms. Silliman in the back of the head with two rounds, blowing off the back of her skull.

The gunman then turned his attention to a horrified Audra Dillon as he began running at her and firing his weapon. Ms. Dillon ran back to her vehicle, managed to get back in the driver's seat and put the car in gear as the windshield and driver's-side door window exploded into shattering glass. The unrelenting gunman continued his violent assault on Ms. Dillon and her vehicle, spraying it with .40-caliber projectiles. Some of the rounds ripped into Ms. Dillon's upper torso, seriously wounding her, as she sped off. Miraculously, Ms. Dillon drove herself to the police station in the village to summon help.

After finishing breakfast and planning our next moves, we returned to the crime scene to brief Sergeant Comanzo on our investigative strategy. Investigators Kevin Garvey and Andy White were assigned to look up Frank Garcia to confirm his whereabouts during the evening and early morning and interview him about his relationship with Mary Silliman. Investigator Scott Walsh and Lieutenant Drew Forsythe were assigned to drive to Albion, New York, which was located outside of Monroe County nearer to Buffalo, to notify Mary Silliman's family of her death and to attempt to locate Jamal Winston to determine his whereabouts at the time of the murder.

While Investigator Peglow was making calls to our Records Division and doing a work-up on the backgrounds of both Jamal Winston and Frank Garcia, I returned to the hospital to see what else I could learn about Frank Garcia, who, as it turned out, was a male Hispanic with a shaved head. Some of the female staff characterized him as a womanizer who used his supervisor status to harass some of the female employees under his charge.

Investigators Garvey and White reported back from the Garcias' residence in less than an hour after leaving the crime scene. Garcia's wife advised them that her husband had not been home all night and was depressed when he left their house the night before. Garcia reportedly called her earlier that morning from his cellphone. He told his wife to watch the news later that day and advised her that she would receive a letter in the mail from him. Mrs. Garcia told the investigators that she was worried about her husband.

She said he was still upset about losing his job at Lakeside hospital and felt he might hurt himself. She did not think her husband would harm anyone except himself. According to Investigator Garvey, Mrs. Garcia was unaware of the shooting at Lakeside hospital.

As a result of this new information, Frank Garcia's stock as a potential suspect spiked. It was crucial that we locate this man as soon as possible and determine his whereabouts at the time of the shooting. Garcia's physical description was consistent with the vague description of the shooter that was provided by the surviving victim. Telling his wife to "watch the news" was a significant fact that we had to follow up on immediately. A double murder was considered newsworthy by anyone's standards.

I eventually met with the Lakeside hospital CEO and director of human resources. Due to the exigent circumstances, they turned over Frank Garcia's personnel file with the agreement that I provide them a subpoena from the district attorney's office as soon as possible. I was looking for anything that might assist us in locating Frank Garcia sooner than later, such as the contact information of personal and professional references he listed on his employment application.

While examining the documents in the file, I located and read a handwritten letter from Mary Silliman that was dated February 5, 2009. The written complaint provided a historical account of how her supervisor, Frank Garcia, had been sexually harassing her over the past several months. Ms. Silliman stated that Frank Garcia had told her how upset he was with another nursing aide on the fourth floor of the nursing home for filing a sexual harassment complaint against him to the hospital administration. This discussion occurred during a smoke break they shared outside the building one night several months prior to the date on Ms. Silliman's letter.

Since that night, they continued to share smoke breaks and talk during their shift. On one occasion, Garcia offered to loan Ms. Silliman the $600 she needed to fix her minivan after she told him it had broken down. Ms. Silliman wrote that she refused the money. A short time after that discussion, Garcia asked Ms. Silliman what she would do for $2,000 besides killing someone. Ms. Silliman wrote that she told Garcia it depended on what the request was.

Then things started to get really weird. During another smoke break, Garcia offered Ms. Silliman $500 to sleep with one of his homegirls. Ms. Silliman wrote that she laughed off the proposal as a joke. However, Garcia showed up at the hospital on one of his nights off and approached her while she was outside smoking during her lunch break. He drove his car up next to Ms.

Silliman and directed her to get inside with him. Once she sat in the front passenger side, Garcia leaned over and tried to kiss her on the mouth. Ms. Silliman said she turned her head away to avoid the kiss and exited his car.

Shortly after Ms. Silliman returned to the building to continue working her shift, she received a text message from Garcia. The text message stated that he was going to "write her up" the next time he worked. Ms. Silliman wrote that she texted Garcia back asking him, "Why?" But he did not answer her. He then sent Ms. Silliman a message, offering her $500 to have sex with him. Ms. Silliman said she refused.

After Garcia returned to work, his propositions got bolder. On one occasion, he had $500 in United States currency spread out on a table in his office when Ms. Silliman walked in. He told her to take the money, but she refused and walked out of the office laughing. Again, she thought Garcia was just messing around with her. During their smoke breaks following that incident, Garcia continued to offer her $500 to "fuck" him or $400 to "suck his dick." She refused. Garcia subsequently offered her more money, first $600, then $700. But Ms. Silliman continued to refuse this predator's steadily more aggressive sexual advances. She eventually grew annoyed and concerned about her supervisor's true intentions toward her, especially when Garcia continued text messaging his propositions during the weekends when he was off from work, asking her if she wanted to make money. Ms. Silliman said she stopped responding to his messages and decided to report the behavior. This was only after she learned Garcia had been doing this to other female staff in the nursing home. Ms. Silliman said she did not report Garcia's boorish actions until early February 2009 because she thought he was just joking around with her. But as his advances became more aggressive and increased in frequency, she realized he was not joking.

After reading Ms. Silliman's letter, I decided that Frank Garcia appeared to be a sexual predator in the workplace who used his authority to coerce female subordinates into having sex with him. It was obvious that Ms. Silliman's complaint against Garcia had something to do with his termination from Lakeside hospital. Whether this caused him to return to the hospital to kill Ms. Silliman as an act of revenge was the question we now had before us. There is a big chasm between the crimes of sexual harassment and murder, but it was not out of the question. I have seen people kill for less when revenge was the motive.

Between Frank Garcia and Ms. Silliman's reportedly abusive live-in boyfriend, Jamal Winston, we had two viable suspects in this case. Each man possessed a motive to kill this woman. Frank Garcia's motive would have been revenge for her refusing his sexual propositions and ultimately filing a complaint against him at work, which most likely caused his termination. Jamal Winston's possible motive was his jealousy and rage over Ms. Silliman's interaction with her male boss at work. Maybe Jamal intercepted one or two of those text messages from Frank Garcia and that fueled his abusive behavior toward her into a murderous rage. However, in light of Frank Garcia's comments to his wife, telling her to watch the news later that day and to check the mail for a goodbye letter, in addition to the predatory behavior that led to his recent termination and subsequent threats to get even with the hospital, it seemed like Garcia was a man in serious trouble or having a mental meltdown. These circumstances led me and other members of the investigative team to believe he was the better candidate of our two potential suspects to be our shooter.

The hospital officials involved in Garcia's termination were concerned for their safety and the safety of their family members and asked for police protection until Garcia was located. The cracks in their voices and the looks on their faces conveyed genuine fear. When Frank Garcia had threatened to get even with them, they had previously interpreted the statement as legal in nature and not a physical threat. Based on what just occurred in the parking lot of their small hospital, the terminated employee's remarks took on an entirely different dimension.

I felt the hospital administrators' concerns were warranted and directed them to the nearby command post for assistance. Until we made contact with Frank Garcia, I was unable to offer these men any comforting words or insight as to whether their concerns held merit. If Frank Garcia was our shooter and was motivated by revenge, would he stop with Silliman's murder? Or did he desire to kill others for what he perceived as an injustice against him? Or would this case be closed by "exceptional clearance" as a result of Garcia putting a bullet in his own head?

Whoever the shooter was, he was proficient with a handgun. And this caused me serious trepidation. The shooter struck Ms. Silliman in the back of the head from a distance of about thirty feet as she was running away from him a millisecond after he had already fatally shot Randall Norman from a slightly longer distance. The fatal shots were not the result of lucky shooting.

What demonstrated to me that we were pursuing an accomplished marksman was the fact that he had placed what appeared to be two rounds in the back of Ms. Silliman's head in a very tight group. Anyone can get lucky with one shot. But to place a tight group of two rounds on a moving target the size of a small melon at thirty feet told me this guy had very good mechanics with respect to sight alignment and trigger control. That level of skilled marksmanship showed me he would be capable of shooting a police officer in the head during a firefight. Our issued bulletproof vests didn't protect us from a headshot. I hoped and prayed that a shootout with the police was not on this guy's list of acceptable scenarios to end this tragic event.

Investigator Peglow and I drove over to the Brockport Village Police Station from the scene about 11:15 a.m. Our hastily conducted background on Garcia produced a cellphone number and address for his sister. I called the number and spoke with a woman who identified herself as Frank Garcia's sister. After identifying myself as a Monroe County Sheriff's investigator, I told the woman we were concerned about her brother's safety and needed to contact him as soon as possible. I purposely did not tell her we suspected that he might have murdered two people and attempted to murder a third.

Garcia's sister was both friendly and cooperative. She advised that he had not stopped by the house that morning or the night before nor had she heard from him. Again, I told her that we needed to speak with her brother as soon as possible and reiterated that we were concerned for his safety. She agreed to give Garcia the message if she heard from him and wrote down my phone number. At my request, she provided me with Garcia's personal cellphone number. I suspected she would reach out to her brother as soon as we hung up, so I decided to give him some time to call me back.

After waiting about fifteen minutes for Garcia to return my call, I dialed his cellphone. Similar to any "knock and talk," where the detective approaches a suspect for the first time in the suspect's own environment, such as the suspect's residence, place of employment or hangout to engage him in conversation about the issue at hand, I was making a "cold call" in an attempt to take Frank Garcia's temperature with respect to his attitude and willingness to meet with me.

In many of these situations, the detective does not know what kind of behavior or attitude the suspect is going to confront him with when that first contact is made. This is where playing detective can be a little dangerous. If we come on too heavy, in an attempt to dissuade the suspect from getting violent with us or resisting arrest, it could cause him to become uncooperative and unwilling to be interviewed. Interviewing the suspect is a very important component of any criminal investigation. It provides us the opportunity to determine whether they are involved in the crime and obtain additional evidence if they are culpable.

Consequently, in certain situations, detectives have to compromise their own personal safety to develop a rapport with a suspect in the hope that he will speak with us voluntarily about the crime for which he is a suspect. Verbal statements from a suspect or person of interest are an important element of an investigation. They allow the detective to calibrate that person relative to their potential culpability. In many instances, an incriminating statement will corroborate other forms of the evidence against a defendant if he is subsequently arrested and charged with a crime.

The detective views an unannounced soft approach of a suspect as a calculated risk, not being reckless with his or her personal safety. It is a skill that is not developed sitting behind a desk in the office. Confronting and engaging people under adversarial conditions for the purpose of getting them to cooperate with you must be practiced carefully and repeatedly.

It comes down to a balancing act similar to walking on a high wire or tiptoeing through a minefield. The detective must appear both casual and relaxed to keep the suspect comfortable and cooperative, choosing their words carefully and controlling their voice flexion and nonverbal communication. However, beneath this façade of personable interaction, they must be prepared to pounce into a physical confrontation at any second and take control of the suspect if he turns aggressive. Practice makes perfect.

How would Frank Garcia react to his first contact with the police? According to the countywide record system, he did not have a police record nor did he have any negative police contacts. Would he even answer his cellphone? And, if he did answer the phone, would he be willing to talk to me or, better yet, meet with me voluntarily? The initial contact would be a low risk since it would take place on the cellphone.

I made the decision to improvise if Garcia answered the call and voluntarily engaged in a conversation with me. My initial plan was to be upfront and honest with him about the shooting and who I was. I figured Garcia possessed some knowledge about Ms. Silliman's abusive live-in boyfriend, Jamal. I was confident the subject must have come up during the many smoke breaks they shared over the past several months. That was where my sincerity and honesty would end.

My plan was to lead Garcia to believe we suspected Jamal for this shooting and considered Garcia and his family to be in imminent danger because of Jamal's jealousy of Garcia's friendship with Ms. Silliman. If I led Garcia to believe he was a suspect it would most likely shut him down from cooperating with me, unless, by chance, he was feeling guilty and remorseful about the murders. The objective was to remain nonaccusatory with my tone and flexible. I would react to his mood and responses. After several rings, a male voice answered Garcia's cellphone.

Frank Garcia confirmed he was the person on the other end of the call. I introduced myself as a member of the Monroe County Sheriff's Office and asked Garcia if he was OK. Sounding apprehensive, Garcia stated he was fine and asked me what was going on. I advised him that one of his former co-workers, Mary Silliman, had just been shot and killed at the hospital and we were concerned for his well-being. I purposely didn't mention the other victims or details of the incident.

As planned, I told Garcia that we believed Ms. Silliman's live-in boyfriend, Jamal Winston, was responsible for the murder because of his jealousy over her friendship with a male co-worker. I told Garcia we suspected he was the male co-worker in question, and I advised him that police officers had been dispatched to his residence to ensure his safety and that of his family until we apprehended Jamal Winston. I said the latter to account for the detectives meeting with his wife and asking questions about his location and status.

Trying to sound as if this was the first time he heard of Ms. Silliman's death, Garcia said he was all twisted up by this tragic revelation. I sensed he was putting on an act—a bad one at that. He made a point of telling me that he and Mary (Silliman) never had a sexual relationship. Feigning concern for his welfare, I told Garcia that I needed to meet with him to make sure he wasn't being held against his will by Jamal Winston and to ask him a few more questions about Mary and Jamal. I reassured Garcia that he would be escorted home safely to be reunited with his family. I told him they would have police protection until we located Jamal.

Garcia agreed with my request; however, he started sniffling as if he was holding back tears. Again, I sensed he was putting on a show not worthy of a B horror flick, but I went along to keep him cooperative. He asked me to allow him some time to gather his composure and process what I had just told him. Not trying to press too hard, I told Garcia that was fine but repeated my concern for him and his family and asked him to get back to me as soon as possible so we could set up a safety plan. Maybe my act was just as bad.

"Until we locate Jamal, I consider you and your family to be in danger," I told Garcia. When I asked him for his location, Garcia told me he was at the beach in Durand-Eastman Park studying in his car. He explained that his laptop computer caught a wireless signal in the areas of Charlotte Beach and Durand-Eastman Beach. Both beach parks are located north of the city along the south shore of Ontario Lake. Garcia said he often parks at these locales to tap into the Internet and study for his college classes.

Garcia told me he was pursuing a master's degree in nursing at Nazareth College in Pittsford, New York, when I asked him what he was studying. I think Garcia knew I was trying to keep him on the phone, for he was hesitant with his answers and sounded distracted. Garcia repeated that he was too upset to talk and needed to hang up. Continuing to convey my concern for his personal safety, I asked him to write down my cellphone number before we disconnected and call me back as soon as possible. Garcia led me to believe he wrote the number down and agreed to call me back.

After I hung up with Garcia, I called Investigator Kevin Garvey, who was with Garcia's wife at their residence. I advised Investigator Garvey of what I told Garcia and asked that he share the same concerns with Mrs. Garcia, just in case he called home to verify my version. Based on the reactions of Garcia and his wife, Investigator Garvey and I agreed something was amiss. Mrs. Garcia appeared to be genuinely concerned for her husband's welfare. We did not believe she possessed any personal knowledge about the shooting or was withholding information about Garcia's whereabouts.

On the other hand, Frank Garcia's behavior was suspicious. Most men would not hesitate to return home in the wake of receiving such alarming information from a police officer. His manner on the phone with me was cagey. He was up to something. We would attempt to lure and coax Garcia into meeting with us by leading him to believe we were focusing on Jamal Winston as our sole suspect. If Garcia was involved in this shooting, we wanted him to believe he got away with murder and was in the clear.

Minutes after we hung up, Investigator Garvey called me back. He advised that Frank Garcia had just called his wife. As she was led to believe by Investigators Garvey and White, Mrs. Garcia told her husband that the police were there to protect her and their children from Jamal Winston.

The groundwork had been laid. Frank Garcia received confirmation from his wife that he was not being pursued as a suspect but as a potential victim. But he remained suspicious and refused to return home immediately. He would only tell his wife that he would eventually come home after he met with Investigator Crough.

Plans were formulated for me to continue calling Garcia's cellphone periodically in order to track his approximate location via the cellphone towers his phone was using to connect with my signal. This process is commonly referred to as "pinging" someone's cellphone to obtain its physical location at that moment in time. It has proven to be a tremendous tool in locating missing persons, potential suspects and fugitives. Investigator Andy White was assigned the task of contacting Verizon, Garcia's cellphone carrier, to provide them with the updated information that was necessary to track Mr. Garcia's cellphone activity. We suspected that the information was going to remain very fluid until Mr. Garcia was located and taken into custody.

I called Garcia's cellphone at noon, but he did not answer, so I left a message asking him to call me back. According to Investigator White, Verizon showed Mr. Garcia's cellphone signal connecting with the tower in Naples, New York, when I was on the phone with him at eleven thirty-one that morning. Naples is located in the heart of the mountainous Finger Lakes Region, approximately forty-five miles south of Rochester in the southern portion of Ontario County, which borders Monroe County along its southern boundary.

The cellphone information confirmed my initial suspicion: Frank Garcia was lying to me. His cellphone signal showed him to be almost an hour's drive from where he said he was. At this point, we were unsure as to why Mr. Garcia was driving through the Naples area. We could only speculate that either he was making a run for it or driving to a secluded location to take his own life. Based on the facts that he had just been fired from his job and told his wife to watch the news and mail for a letter from him, there seemed to be good reason to believe that this case might end as a murder-suicide, a disposition not uncommon in incidents of murder motivated by revenge.

Since I had not heard back from him, I called Garcia's cellphone at about 1:05 p.m. Once again, he did not answer, so I left him a message requesting that he call me back. According to Investigator White, Verizon showed Mr. Garcia's cellphone signal was still connecting with the cell tower in Naples. Maybe he put a round in his head and was dead in his vehicle somewhere in the wilderness south of Canandaigua Lake, I thought.

According to Investigator Garvey, Garcia had called his wife back a second time. Although Garvey was unable to speak with Garcia over the phone, he suspected that Garcia might be feeling us out, quizzing his wife to determine if we were trying to trick him into meeting with us as a pretense to arrest him.

Investigator Garvey said he attempted to speak with Garcia, but Garcia hung up before he was able to engage him in a conversation. Investigator Garvey observed the phone number Garcia was calling his wife from on her phone's caller identification display screen. The number was 727-9641. It was not Garcia's personal cellphone number. Investigator Andy White was assigned to find out the name behind the number.

Everyone on our investigative team had a role to play in this case, especially given the rapid pace in which it was unfolding. As we had many times in the past, the cast of characters in the Monroe County Sheriff's Major Crimes Unit came together and worked as a refined, well-oiled machine. We were working as a team and closing in on our suspect. No one had to tell anyone what to do or what to look for. All of us could play any one of the several constituted roles in a major crime investigation and produce the same result: an arrest followed by a conviction.

It was about 1:20 p.m., and I had not heard back from Frank Garcia, so I called his cellphone again and left him another message asking him to call me back. Until he actually answered the phone, we could only speculate that it was still in his possession and just choosing not to answer our calls.

News that he was using a second cellphone was disconcerting. I decided not to call it because he had not called me from the number. Calling a cellphone number I was not supposed to know existed might have revealed our true motives to Garcia and cause him alarm. We would have to be patient and wait. It was similar to playing a game of chess for very high stakes. We had to anticipate his next move, allowing him some room to operate so as not to expose our goal of locating and detaining him. We knew he already was suspicious of our intentions; therefore, I did not want to provide him additional reasons not to meet with me by calling him on the mysterious cellphone.

Garcia finally called me back from his personal cellphone at about 1:33 p.m. He was polite, apologizing for missing my phone calls. Garcia said his cellphone was off while he was charging its battery. He said he was still in the Charlotte Beach area and was trying to process everything I had told him two hours earlier. Again, knowing Garcia was lying to me, I pressed him to meet with me, reiterating that Jamal Winston was still at large.

Garcia agreed to meet but said he would have to call me right back to set it up and then terminated the call. I checked with Investigator Andy White for the ping location of Garcia's cellphone signal. He advised that Verizon showed Garcia's cellphone signal to be connecting with a tower in the area of 164 Knickerbocker Road in the Pittsford-Mendon area, which is located in southern Monroe County. This information indicated that Garcia was on his way back north. Where had he been for the past several hours, I thought as Investigator White and I hung up.

Minutes later I received a disturbing phone call from Investigator Steve Peglow. He advised that a former female co-worker of Frank Garcia and her husband were found murdered in their residence in Canandaigua, New York. Canandaigua is located in Ontario County, just north of Naples. Based on the information we had been receiving from Verizon regarding Garcia's cellphone location, the killings reportedly occurred during the same time period he was driving around that area of Ontario County.

According to Investigator Peglow, the aforementioned cellphone number (727-9641) that Frank Garcia called his wife from in the presence of Investigators Garvey and White belonged to Kim and Christopher Glatz, the married couple that was found murdered in their Ontario County home. Based on this disturbing information, it became painfully obvious that Garcia had been laying down his own calculated, diabolical scheme to carry out two more murders.

At this point, we also realized Frank Garcia had been "playing us," as we were trying to do the same to him. Was Garcia leading us to believe he was going to meet with me as a ruse to stall for more time so he could murder additional people? Was he going to meet me or was he too suspicious of the police? Or was he orchestrating a potential suicide-by-cop scenario? I pondered these potential outcomes, along with others, as I attempted to digest the tragic news about the Glatz couple and determine our next move.

I decided to stick with the plan. I would continue to act as though we were still pursuing Jamal Winston and were unaware of the murders in Ontario County. As difficult as that would be, I thought leading Garcia to believe he had gotten away with these latest murders was the most conceivable way to get him to meet with me. Unless Garcia communicated he was hip to our plan, I would stay with it. I would have to remain both flexible and steady with my commentary and be ready for any number of reactions from him. That was easier said than done.

I called Garcia's cellphone at about 2:02 p.m. He did not answer, so I left him another message requesting that he call me back. I did my best to not let him hear the trepidation in my voice. Having been a hostage negotiator on our Hostage Rescue Team for nearly twenty years, I had grown accustomed to making such calls—requesting despondent people who were either suicidal or homicidal, or both, to pick up the phone and talk to me.

However, the news of the Glatz murders had shaken my confidence considerably. As I thought about the timeline of that morning and afternoon, it was very apparent to me that I might have been talking to Frank Garcia when he was in the middle of murdering Christopher and Kimberly Glatz or shortly afterward. The man was so cool and collected when we spoke on the phone. While I always suspected Frank Garcia was lying to me, when he portrayed how shaken he was by the news of Mary Silliman's murder, he gave me no indication he was ramped up emotionally or upset with anyone.

To think he was in the midst of murdering two additional people or had just committed the evil deed when we talked told me that we were dealing with someone whose blood had run cold with hatred and was on a premeditated mission of calculated, murderous revenge.

Frank Garcia called me back from his own cellphone five minutes later. Garcia said he was ready to meet with me. His demeanor was cool and cooperative. However, I sensed that he was still suspicious of my intentions. So Garcia would not think I was trying to lure him to a specific location for an ambush-style arrest, I suggested that he choose our meeting place. With that, Garcia suggested the Tim Hortons Restaurant on the corner of Ridge Road and Lake Avenue, in the city of Rochester, saying he was just five minutes from the restaurant.

I told Garcia that I was in Spencerport, several miles west of the location and that it would take me twice the time to get there. After we hung up, I called Sergeant Comanzo and Investigator Garvey to advise them of what had just transpired with Garcia. I then spoke to Investigator White. He advised that Garcia was not lying to me about his current location this time. His cellphone signal showed he was in the Portland Avenue area next to Rochester General Hospital, which is just a short drive to the Tim Hortons that he had suggested.

Garcia called me back from his cellphone about nine minutes later. He asked me for an ETA. In an effort to ease Garcia's concern that he was a suspect and stall for more time so tactical officers could respond to the restaurant and execute a safe arrest, I told him that I had to drive by a couple of addresses in the city to check for Jamal Winston's vehicle before I met with him. I did my best to sound casual regarding our meeting and more focused on arresting Jamal. I knew the tactical officers needed extra time to set up a plan once they arrived in the area.

I told Garcia that I would be delayed and asked him to wait for me. Sounding relaxed and calm, Garcia reassured me he would wait. "That's OK. I'll just get a cup of coffee and chill for a while. I'll be here." I then called Sergeant Comanzo and requested backup from the city police.

By his tone and manner, Garcia sounded confident that he was getting away with what he had done. I believe he felt his meeting with me was going to be a cakewalk. The plan to mislead him into thinking we were pursuing another suspect had worked thus far. Putting off our meeting because I was supposedly checking addresses for Jamal Winston's vehicle had solidified the ruse and removed what suspicion he harbored about my intentions for meeting with him. I wanted him to think of me as a stupid cop he was getting over on. It was my hope that this would lower his guard just enough to allow us the opportunity to get the drop on him without getting someone else shot or killed.

Sergeant Comanzo and I formulated plans to have a team of uniformed tactical officers respond to Tim Hortons and take Garcia down when he exited the restaurant to meet with me. I would serve as bait to get him out of the building to avoid a shootout inside the restaurant or a potential hostage situation. When the officers were in place, I would make a call to Garcia and ask him to come outside to my car, acting as though I was in hot pursuit of Jamal and short on time.

The tactical team could then close in for the arrest. They would also prevent him from getting to his vehicle or running back into the restaurant. Garcia was our suspected shooter, and from what I had observed at the crime scene at Lakeside hospital, he had proven he was well skilled with a handgun. There also was the possibility that he had more than one gun and was wearing a bulletproof vest. We would need to have superior firepower and utilize sound tactics during the takedown to counter these potential hazards.

# ABOUT 2:36 P.M.

As I was cruising eastbound on West Ridge Road toward Tim Hortons on Lake Avenue, I overheard the dispatcher on channel one of my police radio announce that a uniformed officer from the Rochester Police Department had just arrived in the area of Lake Avenue and West Ridge Road. The officer had been assigned to get a visual confirmation that Frank Garcia's green Ford was in the parking lot of the Tim Hortons Restaurant.

About one minute later, I overheard the dispatcher announce that Frank Garcia was in police custody. My mind was filled with both relief and confusion. I knew the tactical team had not yet arrived. What had happened? And how did it go down so fast? These were just a few of the many questions that were going through my mind as I raced to the restaurant. I arrived on scene a couple of minutes after the radio transmission that announced Frank Garcia had been apprehended.

Upon my arrival, I met with the arresting officer, Officer Kevin Koehn, who is the younger brother of Rochester Police lieutenant Jeff Koehn, a dear and close friend of mine. I had never met Officer Koehn until our meeting that afternoon. He provided me a brief synopsis of what happened.

The Tim Hortons Restaurant where Frank Garcia was arrested as he waited for Investigator Patrick Crough to arrive. *Courtesy of Gene Renner.*

At first, Officer Koehn hastily advised me that he had no intention of arresting or even approaching Frank Garcia. As he was directed, Officer Koehn said he drove by the location just to confirm Garcia's vehicle was in the parking lot. As Officer Koehn was rounding the corner slowly in his marked police vehicle and visually scanning the Tim Hortons parking lot, he observed a Hispanic male exit the green Ford and walk slowly toward him with a cup of coffee in his hand as if he had been expecting Officer Koehn.

Like any good and brave street cop, Officer Koehn quickly exited his vehicle to confront Frank Garcia. Officer Koehn calmly instructed Garcia to put his hands where he could see them and then disarmed him of his Glock .40-caliber semiautomatic pistol. Once handcuffed by Officer Koehn, Frank Garcia was placed in the back of Officer Koehn's police car without incident.

I assured Officer Koehn that I was not mad and did not consider his actions as careless or reckless. In fact, I considered him to be a hero and thanked God that he had not been shot by this mutt. As in this instance, sometimes police officers are confronted with situations out of their control and have to respond within a split second the best way they know how based on their training and experience—even when backup has yet to arrive.

Officer Koehn's actions were commendable and professional—textbook. Had Officer Koehn responded to Frank Garcia's casual advance toward his police car in a different manner, it could have resulted in a firefight with a formidable opponent who had already demonstrated that he was a very good shot with his handgun.

I believe Frank Garcia mistakenly thought Officer Koehn was, in fact, me arriving at the restaurant for our meeting. That would explain why he got out of his vehicle with his cup of cappuccino in hand when he observed the police car slowly driving by the parking lot. It was as if Garcia was trying to get Officer Koehn's attention. (Garcia later confirmed he thought I was Officer Koehn, for he did not realize he had been talking to an investigator and not a uniformed officer when we spoke on the phone.)

There must have been ten Rochester Police officers on the scene within a minute of my arrival. Some had arrived before me. I needed to get our suspect away from all the commotion. I spoke briefly with Rochester Police lieutenant Frank Umbrino, the highest-ranking command officer at the scene and made arrangements with him about securing the suspect's vehicle and handgun until our crime scene evidence technicians arrived to take custody of them.

I then asked Officer Koehn to transport Garcia downtown to the Public Safety Building while I followed in my unmarked police car. Upon our arrival, Garcia, who was handcuffed behind his back, was escorted via elevator to the fourth floor of the building, where the Monroe County Sheriff's Office Criminal Investigation Section is located. After a short hike to the northeast corner of the fourth floor, where the Major Crimes Unit is housed, Frank Garcia was placed in Interview Room no. 2.

I removed Officer Koehn's handcuffs and placed my handcuffs on Garcia. I then cuffed him to the chair where he was sitting. After I completed a visual scan of the room for potential contraband left behind from another case, we exited the room, leaving Garcia to his own thoughts.

I studied our suspect on the computer monitor of the digital recording system in a room adjacent to the interview rooms. The Major Crimes Unit interview rooms are monitored by audio and visual recording equipment. All custodial interviews are recorded directly onto the hard drive of a computer located in an electronic equipment storage room.

Garcia, wearing blue jeans and a camouflage sweatshirt, was slouched in one of the two chairs next to the small round table in the room. Handcuffed to the chair, he stared at the floor or straight ahead. His head was shaved smooth. His skin was light brown. His piercing dark eyes sat below thick brown eyebrows that appeared to be in a constant furrow.

Officer Koehn and I returned to the interview room five minutes later to conduct a second physical search of Garcia. I have no doubt that Officer Koehn's search at the scene of the arrest was thorough, but we could not afford to take any chances with this suspect. Unfortunately, it is not out of the realm of possibilities to miss a second weapon during a hasty pat-down search at the time of an arrest, especially when the most obvious weapon is found or surrendered. Mistakes happen, sometimes with fatal results.

Every police department has suffered their share of mishaps when it comes to suspects not being properly searched and later found to have a knife or handgun while seated in an interrogation room or holding cell. Police officers have been shot, and suspects have taken their own lives while in police custody. I've seen police videos depicting these tragic scenarios. Complacency is every cop's enemy. Being distracted during a search of a suspect can easily turn into a fatal error. When conducting a physical search of a suspect for weapons, we must always stay focused on the mission at hand.

Officer Koehn said he was the only person who searched Frank Garcia at the time of his arrest. In my opinion, every suspect should be searched twice. After being searched by the arresting officer, the suspect should be searched a second time by a different officer. I conducted the second search while Officer Koehn stood by.

I located and removed Garcia's inside-the-pants-style holster for his .40-caliber Glock semiautomatic pistol, a tactical style belt that is made and worn for the purpose of carrying concealed handguns, and several bullets from his front pants pocket. We then exited the interview room and left Mr. Garcia alone again. I handed the items confiscated to Officer Koehn and requested that he catalog each on a Property Custody Report and then secure them as evidence.

I returned to the interview room about eight minutes later and sat down next to the small round table opposite a tense Frank Garcia. I proceeded to advise Garcia of his Miranda warnings by reading them verbatim from a rights waiver form.

"Am I a suspect?" Garcia interrupted me.

"You're a person of interest because you had a relationship with this woman." I was referring to Mary Silliman.

"But I didn't have a relationship with her," he insisted.

"Well, you had some kind of relationship with her at work. We're looking for Jamal Winston, too. OK?" I said, trying to not piss him off.

"Please find him," he pleaded. "I don't want him around my house, especially cause I'm here."

"No problem," I responded. "We thought this might be a feud between you and him. I have to ask you about your relationship with him [Jamal]. Fair enough?"

"Yeah," said Garcia.

He was still playing along with my charade about Jamal Winston being the shooter. That was a good thing. Thus far he believed we were still focusing on someone else and not him. I needed Garcia to remain cooperative and voluntarily waive his rights so I could continue the interview. I could tell it was going to be a difficult undertaking once he realized there was no other suspect. He was already jumpy and slightly agitated about being in our custody.

I continued, "Anytime somebody's in custody, we have to read them their rights, but you're just a person of interest."

"Yeah," Garcia said.

"OK. Kapeesh?" I said, trying to keep him cooperative.

"OK," Garcia answered.

"You have the right to remain silent. And I'm saying this to you because you're in custody."

"Uh-huh," Garcia acknowledged.

I continued, "Anything you say can and will be used against you in a court of law."

"Uh-huh," he answered.

I continued reading from the rights waiver form. "You have the right to talk to a lawyer and to have him present while you're being questioned," I said.

"Uh-huh," he answered.

"If you cannot afford to hire a lawyer, one will be appointed to represent you before any questioning if you wish. You can decide at any time to exercise your rights and not answer any questions or make any statements," I said. "Do you understand that?"

"Uh-huh," Garcia responded.

"Is that a yes?" I asked

"Yes, OK," Garcia answered.

I continued. "Having these rights in mind, do you wish to talk to me now with the understanding you can stop at anytime?"

"Yeah, but I am a person of interest, right?" Garcia asked.

"Yes," I answered.

"So I don't think there is anything for me to get a lawyer for because I'm not being charged with anything, so it's OK," he said.

"So is that a yes?" I asked.

"Yes," he answered.

I wrote down his answers to the two waiver questions and put the rights waiver form aside. I started out by asking Garcia about his education and current employment status. He advised that he was currently attending Nazareth College, working on his master's degree in nursing. Nazareth is a small but very reputable college located in Pittsford, New York. Garcia said he was recently terminated by Lakeside hospital but had seventeen years' experience as a nurse. His specialty was geriatric care.

I found his initial explanation for the termination from Lakeside to be ambiguous. He said it had something to do with his education and not having enough contact with the patients. I didn't push him for clarification, for I did not want to alienate him. We were just getting started. I wanted to get as much of this guy on the recording as possible. As soon as Garcia asked for a lawyer, it would be over. So I didn't want to piss him off just yet.

I wasted no time getting to the first issue at hand: his personal relationship with Mary Silliman. Garcia maintained that he never had a sexual relationship with her.

"There wasn't any relationship. She used to come and get me to smoke. We were smoking buddies," he said.

"Smoking buddies?" I asked.

"She used to talk," Garcia said.

"Did she confide in you?" I asked.

"No, only when I asked her a couple times when she had marks on her back; but, you know, I am her supervisor. I had to be careful with the role, passing back and forth because I got to maintain that line there," he said while drawing an imaginary line in the air between us. "I used to ask her, where are the bruises from? She really wasn't saying anything about it."

Garcia said the bruises he observed on Ms. Silliman were located on her left shoulder and neck area. Again, he insisted she never confided in him about how she obtained the bruises. "No, I never went deeper because I had to maintain that line. She's a subordinate. I am a supervisor. I had to maintain that line," he repeated.

Garcia denied ever meeting Jamal Winston or speaking with him. I challenged his repeated statement that he never "crossed the line" with Ms. Silliman by confronting him about text messaging Ms. Silliman on her cellphone when she was not at work. I told Garcia that Jamal might have intercepted those text messages and got angry with her.

Garcia admitted sending her text messages when she was not working but stated they were harmless and nonsexual. "I came out of a vagina. I'm not trying to get my whole life back in one. It's overrated, especially me being in nursing," he said.

Garcia said he had worked too hard for everything he has to put it at risk over having a sexual relationship with one of his female subordinates. "I ain't going to waste it over two labias, minora and two majoras and…"

"Labias? What did you call them?" I asked

"Labias, that's what they call them," he answered. "That's what they call them. Labia minora, majora and clitoris and mouse hairs. I ain't going to waste everything over that."

This arrogant and vulgar man would not fare well with female jurors after they watched and heard him make this type of statement, degrading the female gender. This was the beauty of video and audio recording interviews and interrogations of suspects. The judge and jury get to see and hear firsthand exactly how the defendant acted with the police and what they said. Good stuff.

All I wanted to do was keep Frank Garcia talking. He did not know he was on "candid camera." Whether he ever admitted to the crimes, his lies were going to add up against him and help prove his guilt. I chose not to press Garcia for the truth at that point in the interview and just allowed him to bury himself in the deceit of his exculpatory statements that would be used against him in court.

I did this because I was fairly certain that Garcia would become angry with me and ask for a lawyer if and when I confronted him for the truth. Garcia still believed we were pursuing Jamal Winston and assumed he was going to be released after we spoke. I knew as time wore on it was going to become crystal clear to him that he had been duped into meeting with me. And that was going to make him very upset.

I patiently sat back and kept giving our suspect more rope to ultimately hang himself. The arrogant and prideful Frank Garcia liked to feel as though he was in control and the smartest guy in the room. I continued to oblige Garcia in that regard, allowing him the opportunity to step all over himself.

# THERE IS NO GREATER LOVE THAN TO LAY DOWN ONE'S LIFE FOR ONE'S FRIENDS

## *John 15:13 (NLT)*

While I was interviewing Garcia, my colleagues were collaborating with detectives from the Ontario County Sheriff's Office. It was paramount that

City of Canandaigua, New York. The Glatzes lived just outside the city. *Courtesy of Gene Renner.*

we gathered details about the Glatz murders in Canandaigua, New York, so I could question Garcia about his suspected involvement.

The usual procedure with interviewing suspects is the detective who commences the interview continues the interview until it results in either a confession or the suspect terminates the interview. A swap would occur only if the decision was made that there might be a personality clash between the suspect and lead interviewer and it would be advantageous to put someone else in there.

Detectives from other police departments and jurisdictions eventually can be introduced to the suspect, if they remain cooperative, to gather more details of the crimes committed by the suspect in their respective jurisdictions. The standard practice in our law enforcement community is to provide the lead interviewing detective information about each crime the suspect is suspected of committing. They then question the suspect about each incident and attempt to get at least an admission and a minimum account of the suspect's involvement in each crime.

Detectives from the other departments and jurisdictions can glean more details from the suspect about their respective crimes when the lead interviewer is finished with the suspect—if they are still cooperating. If things go south, the suspect has hopefully already copped to the crimes in question, at least made some type of incriminating statements or told lies that contradict the physical evidence collected at the crime scene and witness testimony during their interview with the lead detective.

The goal is to keep the interview fluid and the suspect cooperative. The lead interviewer most likely has already established a rapport with the suspect and should be the only person speaking to them until business has been completed. Introducing a second or third detective into the interview prematurely can potentially cause more harm than good. As it has been said, too many cooks in the kitchen at one time can make for a shitty pot of soup.

Mrs. Glatz had two children from a previous marriage, a fourteen-year-old daughter, *Heather, and thirteen-year-old son, *Shane. Both children were present in the family's residence when their parents were murdered execution style. What these two children had been subjected to at the hands of this evildoer was horrific. To know that I was talking with Frank Garcia on the cellphone as he was terrorizing this poor family still turns my stomach and causes me heartache. Even though we know Garcia was at the Glatzes' residence an hour prior to my first contact with him, a part of me will always feel as though I failed them in some way.

According to the children, their Valentine's Day Saturday morning was disrupted by a strange man who had entered their home about 10:30 a.m. Both children were upstairs when they heard yelling coming from the first-floor living room area, where the front entrance of the home was located.

Mrs. Glatz called her daughter downstairs. Heather observed a man standing at the bottom of the stairs as she descended to the first floor. He was a light-skinned, Hispanic-looking black male somewhere between thirty and forty years old who was cleanshaven and baldheaded. The man was brandishing a black handgun that he continued to wave around. He was upset with the Glatzes, especially Mrs. Glatz, saying something about the hell he went through and some letters. Heather overheard her stepfather refer to the man as "Frankie."

Heather noticed the man was wearing a gold wedding band that had diamonds across it. This proved to be a keen observation that helped corroborate her subsequent positive identification of him as the person who murdered her parents that fateful morning.

Frank Garcia eventually told Heather to take care of her brother, who suffers from cerebral palsy and can't walk. Heather bravely prepared breakfast for her younger sibling in the midst of this unfolding nightmare. Garcia then directed Heather to fix him some toast and butter and asked for a glass of water. When he finished his toast, Garcia told Heather to clean his glass and coffee cup that he had used as an ashtray for his cigarettes. He also ordered her to wash his cigarette butts down the drain of the kitchen sink.

The fact that Garcia was ordering the young girl to clean up after him and destroy his smoked cigarettes tells me he did not want to leave behind any trace evidence that would lead the police back to him. This behavior indicates that his initial plan must have included him murdering everyone in the Glatz residence that morning. And he was taking the necessary precautions to increase his chances of getting away with the gruesome crimes. These were the actions of a cold and calculated person who had premeditated intentions.

Heather was then directed by Garcia to return to her brother's room after he promised her nothing was going to happen. While in Shane's room, Heather turned the volume of the radio up so he wouldn't hear what was happening. Both children could overhear Garcia ordering Chris Glatz to write down the names and addresses of their parents and siblings. At one point, Heather heard Garcia demand $25,000 from her mother and stepfather. She overheard Chris Glatz ask Garcia if he would leave if they got him the money.

"No, somebody has to die," Garcia answered. He threatened to kill the Glatzes' relatives if they didn't send the money to his wife. Garcia said it was for her because he wasn't going to be around much longer.

At some point during the terror and confusion that morning, Garcia ordered Chris Glatz to move Garcia's green Ford from the street into the driveway. He told Glatz that if he did not return he would kill everyone in the house. Glatz did as he was told. After moving Garcia's vehicle into their driveway, he returned to the house without giving it a second thought. When I first heard of this selfless act of courage, I got choked up with emotion and deep admiration. I never met this man, but I think of him often. And I hope and pray that I could display such courage and sacrifice if confronted with similar hopeless circumstances.

When most people would run from such danger, Chris Glatz chose to run right back at it, knowing he was going to be killed. Garcia had told them he already killed three people that morning. Frank Garcia was a man who had nothing to lose. He had already committed himself to the point of no return. Therefore, the likelihood of Garcia making good on his threats that someone had to die was very high.

Essentially, Chris Glatz voluntarily dove on a live grenade in an attempt to save others—and he did. He saved the children's lives. I believe Frank Garcia would have killed everyone in that house and then publicly displaced the blame on Chris for not returning to the house if Chris had chosen not to return.

No one would have faulted Chris Glatz had he decided to run to the neighbors to call 911 and let the police take over. That would have been the prudent and logical thing to do. No one would fault someone for running away from a live grenade to avoid suffering serious injury or even death. Diving onto it goes against all logic and our nature to stay alive. Chris Glatz could have avoided his death but chose otherwise and made the ultimate sacrifice. He will forever be remembered as a hero.

Heather overheard her mother plead with Garcia to let them live. She heard her mother plead for her husband's life, asking Garcia to kill only her. She overheard Garcia ask her stepfather if he wanted his casket to be open or closed. With brave defiance, Heather stepped out of her brother's room, confronting Garcia on her mother and stepfather's behalf. "You promised me that nothing was going to happen!" she said. Garcia acknowledged the promise but told the courageous young girl that he had to go back on it. He then ordered her to leave the room. Heather said she knew right then that he was going to shoot them.

Garcia could be heard asking Chris Glatz if he wanted to be shot in the stomach or head. Both Mr. and Mrs. Glatz begged him, for their children's sake, not to take their lives. Mrs. Glatz became desperate as she retrieved her sick son from his bedroom and carried him out to the living room to show Garcia that Shane needed them to care for him. Shane even begged Garcia not to kill his parents.

"Do you want me to shoot your dog and spare your parents?" Garcia asked the boy.

"I don't want anyone to die!" Shane pleaded.

"Good answer," Garcia said coldly. He then ordered Chris Glatz to carry the boy back to his bedroom.

"I don't want him to see me shoot you."

Chris Glatz courageously said goodbye to his stepson and returned to the living room, knowing what fate awaited him. Garcia could be overheard telling them to lay facedown on the two sofas in the room.

From Shane's bedroom, both of Kimberly Glatz's children heard a gunshot and her mother crying and asking to hold her husband as he slowly died.

"No," Garcia coldly replied.

Heather cried out. Garcia came into the bedroom and ordered her to keep quiet. Then the children heard two more shots. Garcia returned to

Shane's bedroom for a second time and ordered the hysterical and frightened children to keep quiet, threatening to shoot them if they didn't do so. Garcia returned to the room several more times. Sometimes he would just look at them and not say anything.

One of the times he came into the room, he said, "If you have the same bad gene pool as your parents then I should kill you now."

"Is my mom OK?" Heather asked.

"She's alright," said Garcia. "You can talk to her after I leave."

Garcia toyed with their minds as he openly contemplated whether to kill them or not. "I don't shoot kids," he said.

"I don't trust you. You hurt Chris after you said you wouldn't," Heather courageously retorted.

"You want to die?" Garcia asked them.

Both children pleaded for their lives.

"I'll have to think about it," Garcia said as he walked out of the room.

Frank Garcia returned to Shane's bedroom within minutes after telling the children that he had to think about whether he was going to kill them. I could not imagine the horror those children were experiencing as they awaited their fate. The world they knew had just been shattered.

Garcia informed the children that he would let them live but made it contingent on their cooperation. He made them promise that they would not identify him to the police. Young Shane offered to tell the police that he was asleep the entire time. Garcia took the list of family members with him, along with the cellphone batteries and chargers. He even placed a clock in their bedroom and ordered the children to give him twenty minutes before they exited the bedroom. Garcia told the children that he would have his people hunt them and their family members down and kill them all if the children gave him up to the police or exited the bedroom before the twenty minutes had expired.

Once he finally left the residence, the children did as they were told. Waiting the twenty minutes felt like a second eternity to the one they had just endured.

Heather then exited her brother's bedroom and walked into the living room. She observed her mother and stepfather to be lying facedown on separate sofas. She tried to wake her mom, hoping and praying she was still alive. There was no response. Panic-stricken, Heather quickly made her way over to the neighbor's house and asked them to use the phone. The first call she made was to her daddy, Christopher Fonda, a deputy sheriff of the Ontario County Sheriff's Office.

41

Kimberly and Christopher Glatz had been shot to death execution style after they were forced to lay facedown on their sofas. Pillows were used to muffle the gunshots and contain the explosive damage caused by the high-powered .40-caliber round that was fired at point-blank range.

These two children were well cared for and loved by many members of the three families they are part of. Their youthful innocence was ripped away by a person who did not possess a soul. Both of them showed remarkable courage and resilience with the way they confronted a strange and scary armed man hellbent on murdering everyone in their home.

When one investigates incidents such as this case on a frequent basis, there usually isn't enough time to ponder the devastation that perpetrators inflict on others as a result of their selfish and evil actions. I believe it has always been a coping mechanism that allowed me to continue my work with a clear mind. Now that I am removed from the daily grind of being immersed in one major case after another, I have time to reflect.

I find myself thinking about all the victims and their families and what it must have felt like to suffer as a result of the senseless, evil acts of another and the immeasurable sense of loss, anger and rage they continue to feel. To lose a loved one to an accident or terminal disease would be difficult enough. But to lose someone you care about and love more than life itself because some lowlife with an indifference to the sanctity of human life caused their untimely, and many times horrific, death is too much for anyone to bear.

Frank Garcia continued to deny any knowledge or involvement in the shootings at Lakeside hospital. He continued to deny any type of sexual harassment behavior toward Mary Silliman and insisted it had nothing to do with him being terminated by the hospital. We had learned otherwise.

Garcia proudly talked about his stint as a military policeman in the New York National Guard and his deep sense of patriotism for this country.

"And I wouldn't waste that over a vagina," Garcia said.

"Over a vagina?" I asked. Because our conversation was being recorded I wanted him to elaborate.

"I would waste it for self-defense," he explained, "to protect my two little ones and my wife but not for vagina."

Garcia was becoming increasingly agitated with me as I asked him a second time where he was that early morning and the following hours that led into the afternoon.

"Were you anywhere near the hospital early this morning?" I asked.

"No," Garcia insisted. He said he left his residence at eight o'clock the night before and drove to Charlotte Beach to pick up the wireless signal on his laptop computer. He remained there studying until about eleven that evening. Garcia said he then drove to the Lakeshore Nursing Home where he met up with one of the female staff members he would only identify as one of his homegirls. After he hung out with the mystery woman for a while, Garcia said he returned to Charlotte Beach, where he played computer games on his laptop and then took a nap. Again, Garcia insisted he was at Charlotte Beach when I called him later that morning and remained there until he met with me in the afternoon.

Knowing what I knew, I looked at Garcia's explanation of his whereabouts as nothing more than lies and fragmented gibberish. He refused to identify who his homegirl was despite my pressing him for her name so we could verify his account of being with her.

"There's something odd that I am curious about," I said. "Your wife said when you left her last you told her to 'Watch the news.' What was that all about?"

"I never said that to her," Garcia insisted, shifting in his seat. He suggested that his wife had earwax in her ears, causing her to hear him wrong. Then he directed the conversation back to him leaving the house to drive around until he was able to locate a wireless signal with his laptop computer.

"Is there anything in your work file that you should be concerned about with respect to this?" I asked Garcia. I was referring to his interaction with Mary Silliman and her written complaint against him for sexual harassment.

"No," he replied.

"No indication that you had a relationship with her?" I asked him again.

"No, no." he insisted.

"There's nothing in your file that would indicate you guys had what you'd deem as an inappropriate relationship?" I asked again.

He was obviously lying, so I wanted to make sure there was no doubt that he was a liar by asking the same question more than once, allowing him more than one chance to tell the truth. I wanted to remove all doubt that Frank Garcia understood the question and was intentionally lying.

Again, I was thinking ahead to what the judge would be viewing at a suppression hearing and what a jury would be viewing at trial. Despite Garcia's protests, I continued my routine of repeating questions regarding evidentiary issues. The evidence was going to prove he was a murderer. His recorded interview was going to prove him to be a bona fide liar.

"I already answered that a couple minutes ago," Garcia said, growing annoyed with me. "I just want to get out of here," he grumbled. "I'm answering all your questions. I am being compliant, and I'm not asking for my attorney."

"You have been," I said, trying to keep him cooperative. "You're being very compliant, and I appreciate that immensely. I'm not—"

Garcia cut me off. "I got my car taken away. I got my arm taken away. I got my mags taken away. I got locked in the back of a small Impala. I mean, I'm treated like a suspect—I hate these handcuffs!"

I tried to sooth Garcia's damaged ego. I appealed to his training and experience as a military cop, suggesting he should know that his being handcuffed was just a matter of procedure.

I probed him with another question. "Is there something going down we need to know about?"

"I already answered that like fifteen minutes ago," said Garcia, growing more irritated with each additional question. "Like I said, I don't throw away everything I've worked for, just for a vagina."

"OK, OK," I responded, my tone conveying empathy, "Let me make a phone call and get back to you."

I knew this duel of charades we were playing against one another was eventually going to end. Garcia was upset he wasn't winning. His compounded lies were collapsing like a house of cards. The realization that he was tricked into voluntarily meeting with me was starting to settle in and fueled his anger. Other than his repeated denials, Garcia refused to engage in any substantive conversation about his involvement in any of the murders.

Garcia began lamenting about his gun and car being taken away from him and wanted to know when he was going to get them back. He also advised me that he had been attending a local pistol range, practicing how to shoot defensively and tactically—similar to the way police officers train on a pistol range. I considered this statement to be incriminating since it corroborated Garcia possessed the skill to shoot his weapon proficiently. It would account for the shooter's deadly accuracy that was displayed at the Lakeside hospital double murder scene.

I excused myself from the interview room, telling Garcia that I was going to see when I could get him home. Continuing to pretend that I was sympathetic to his concerns about being detained, I told Garcia that I was going to check on the status of Jamal Winston.

Frank Garcia stared at me intensely as I walked back into the interview room and took my seat. He was emotionally coiled up as tight as a rattlesnake just before it strikes. When I attempted to engage him in conversation, he unleashed his wrath.

"I'm being treated like a fucking criminal here!" he blurted out, "I ain't no fucking criminal just because I smoked with her. Hell, I've worked hard to get where I'm at. Treated like a damn criminal! I ain't no damn criminal. I paid my dues to society! I served my damn country! I hate these damn handcuffs!"

As I had anticipated, the interview started to deteriorate when I pressed Garcia for answers to questions regarding evidentiary issues and his whereabouts that morning—he wasn't having any of it. The first question related to the Glatzes' cellphone number that he called his wife from while she was in the presence of the other detectives. I referred to the phone number by the numerals only, making no reference to the Glatzes.

I asked Garcia where he called his wife from the one time he didn't call her from his own cellphone, when the police were with her.

"Pay phone," he responded.

"Pay phone?" I asked. "That's what you called her from?"

"Yeah," Garcia answered

"OK. Where was the pay phone, do you remember?" I asked. "Was it the 727 number? Is that a pay phone? Because she showed the cops the number."

"I'm not sure," he responded. "I know it was on the Ridge, but…" Garcia was referring to Ridge Road, which is located in the northern portion of Monroe County, miles and miles away from the Glatzes' residence.

"You can tell me," I said. "I can have the phone company narrow that down and boom, we're all set." I knew he would not be able to provide me with that information since he was stacking one lie on top of the other. The fact was that there was no pay phone. He knew I was referring to the Glatzes' cellphone.

Garcia's response was nothing but babble as he rambled on how we can't trust the numbers that are displayed on our cellphone screens.

"OK. So you're saying you called from a pay phone?" I asked him again.

"Yeah," he responded, again.

This set of lies regarding his use of the Glatzes' cellphone would prove beneficial to the prosecution of Garcia in his Ontario County murder trial. We had him dead nuts using the Glatzes' cellphone right around the time of their murders. Garcia admitted that he called his wife from the 727 number. He then bolstered the incriminating admission with a lie, identifying the Glatzes' cellphone number as a pay phone in northern Monroe County. This lie was monumental, in my opinion. It demonstrated that Garcia knew the cellphone would connect him to the Glatzes and implicate him as their murderer. An innocent person would have no reason to lie about such a matter.

A partial admission of what appears to be an innocuous fact that could connect someone to a crime can be, in some instances, considered unremarkable. However, when the suspect attempts to neutralize the admission with a lie, it ends up being an unintended affirmation of guilt. Lying always indicates someone is hiding something. When a person lies to cover up or rationalize evidence of their potential involvement in a crime it screams "guilty." A proven lie is as good as an admission of guilt.

Garcia showed no remorse or hesitation with his repeated denials and lazy excuses and explanations. His self-serving behavior demonstrated just how evil and calloused he was.

When I showed Frank Garcia Mary Silliman's handwritten letter that complained about his sexual harassment of her, he claimed it was a forgery, refusing to even look at it. Garcia insisted it was all "bullshit" and maintained that he was fired because he didn't meet the hospital's standards.

When I asked Garcia if he had ever been in the Canandaigua or Farmington areas that day he adamantly denied it, claiming he had not been in either of those areas over the past year.

"I answered all your questions!" Garcia blurted out impatiently. "Can we go?"

Trying to keep the interview going, I changed the topic to Jamal Winston.

"They're talking to Jamal right now," I offered.

"I don't care about him or his goons, even though I am unarmed right now!" Garcia shot back.

Changing the topic to defuse his hostility I asked, "Well, you can understand why we want to check the ballistics?"

"Yeah, yeah, I know that," Garcia stated. Then he said, "Ballistics is not even accurate anyways."

"It's not?" I asked.

Garcia said, "No, not really. The twist on all those shells from Glock autos is all the same."

"Oh, they are?" I asked, attempting to sound surprised so as to lead him to believe he was educating me about something I didn't know.

Garcia had just made another serious error, in my opinion. The fact that he knew how the rifling marks left on the projectiles fired from Glock pistols were uniform in nature and difficult to tell apart was significant. I believe this knowledge led to why he chose to use such a weapon to commit the murders. Most handguns and long guns leave their own identifying marks on the projectile from the grooving on the inside of the barrel. The gun barrels of Glock semiautomatic pistols rarely leave a signature mark on the projectile.

I decided to burst Garcia's bubble of confidence in his perceived belief that we would not be able to connect his gun to the crime scene.

"What about the casings?" I asked, referring to the empty shell casings left behind by the shooter at the scene of the Lakeside hospital murders.

"Bullets, bullets—they come a dime a dozen," Garcia answered. I realized he had no idea what I was talking about or the significance.

"The casings," I said. "We can determine if they came from a specific gun." It was obvious from his perplexed look and ambiguous response to my remark about the shell casings left behind by the shooter, Garcia had no idea what I was talking about. He did not know the markings left on spent shell casings by the extractor rods of the pistol they were fired from could be traced back to that respective weapon.

Garcia continued to stumble around the issue of the shell casings, trying to make sense of what he had just learned. I could tell his confidence was giving way to frustration, sending him into a mental and emotional tailspin.

"Crough, please—leave me alone. I am having a nervous breakdown here. Even though I know I am innocent," Garcia groaned. Then he switched the subject. "You're going to send me out there with my pants around my knees and my underwear down," he protested. "I am an American—I have obligations!"

"We'll give you your belt back," I said. I knew Garcia was referring to us not giving him his handgun back. But I decided to toy with him a little to keep him off balance.

"No, no. I'm not talking about that!" he retorted. "I'm talking about my arms. The whole point is you take me out there with my pants down—who cares about that damn belt! I have a different belt!"

"Well, I thought you meant I was going to literally make you walk out with your pants down."

"You're leaving me naked!" Garcia lamented.

"Without your gun?" I finally acknowledged. I didn't want to send him over the edge.

"Yeah," Garcia answered. "I am an American. I have an obligation to be armed at all times, personal protections, protect myself, my family or I see the commission of a felony in action. That's the American way; that's the patriotic way to do things."

"Right," I responded. He took a breath.

"I'm a real American. I'm a real American. My shoes are made in America. I am a patriot!" he exclaimed. Garcia then mentioned Mary Silliman's letter again, demanding that I tell him who really wrote it. I offered to let him read it for himself, but he refused to even look at the document and told me it was irrelevant.

I pressed Garcia about the $600 Silliman said he offered her for sex.

"Let's not play games," he snapped.

"I'm not playing games," I responded.

"I will shut up, do the Fifth, Sixth—whatever—and get the hell out of here!" he threatened. Garcia knew I would back off to keep him cooperative. He needed some breathing room so he could formulate his next lies.

"You gave me your word you were going to get me the hell out of here," he snarled.

"I said only after they talk to Jamal," I corrected him.

"Who cares about him?" he shot back.

"Listen, I—"

Garcia cut me off. "I wasn't there! I wasn't near the vicinity! I wasn't even there, man!"

He then rebuked me for the way I convinced him to meet with me. "Maybe I should've stood my ground. My stomach is churning. What the fuck did you call me for? You told me I was in danger."

Garcia was upset that he had been bamboozled. He was upset that we confiscated all his guns. He was upset that we were looking at him as the shooter.

Again, I tried to downplay his complaint and get his emotions off the ceiling by changing the topic of discussion. I eventually engaged him in conversation about one of his favorite things: handguns.

"You like that Glock?" I asked, referring to the semiautomatic pistol that he was found to be in possession of at the time of his arrest and suspected of using in the murders that morning. I told Garcia that the H&K .40-caliber pistol we carried had a bit of a kick to it. I also made reference to the .357 magnum revolver and Smith & Wesson 9 mm we used to carry as our service weapon.

"Are you getting in my mind?" Garcia shot back.

"No, no," I answered, trying to reassure him I wasn't playing mind games with him. Garcia was picking up on my tactic of engaging him in idle conversation when I wanted to calm him down. However, I wanted him to talk about his weapon to demonstrate how knowledgeable he was with firearms.

"Or do you really want to know?" Garcia asked, skepticism still in his voice.

"Yeah, yeah," I answered.

"The way you avoid that is you put rubber grips on it," Garcia said, referring to how I could reduce the kick of recoil when I fired my weapon. He couldn't avoid the opportunity to be the smartest guy in the room.

"Rubber grips?" I asked.

"Yeah, yeah—like holds the fingers steadier. Rest the thumb on the block," he said, clarifying his point.

I told him that when I came on the job we carried the .38-caliber revolver and then converted to the Smith & Wesson .357 magnum revolver shortly after I graduated from the police academy. I told Garcia I enjoyed shooting the .357.

"That's too powerful" he said. "It's heavy."

I advised Garcia that the department was going to convert to a .45 Glock semiautomatic pistol in the near future, which would make it my fifth handgun we've transitioned to since I got on the job. Again, he was compelled to demonstrate his superior knowledge about handguns.

"If somebody is on cocaine," he began, "you have to knock them out a couple times with that .45 because they won't feel the shot. The velocity is slow. You hit them with a .40, you get maybe four hundred feet per pound, per second, faster."

"OK," I said

"The .40 is a combination of speed and knockdown power." He spoke with both authority and confidence.

"Gotcha," I thought.

"All my security teams, all my security at Water Street, have it." he offered, referring to a private security detail he allegedly supervised at a local concert hall in the city. It was the first time Garcia had mentioned anything about working as an armed private security guard. I decided to probe a little further.

"Oh, you work there?" I asked.

"I know all them—the ones at the mags and the security—they all have .40s," he said. I found his response to be ambiguous. I was confused as to whether he worked there but chose not to make an issue of it. I interpreted it as an attempt to elevate his status to that of a law enforcement officer, presenting himself as my equal.

As much as I desired to confront this self-anointed modern-day warrior and crusader about his lies and unleash a verbal assault upon him, I knew such a move would deflate his puffed-up, fragile ego. His attitude was already that of a brittle wire, ready to break from the least amount of pressure or confrontation from me. My experience and instincts as an interrogator told me that turning the interview confrontational would surely shut Garcia down and cause him to demand his lawyer.

While Garcia wasn't admitting to anything related to the murders, I was receiving small dividends for my patience. He was unwittingly providing me good information as to why he liked to use the .40 Glock pistol to shoot people. It was the same gun as our suspected murder weapon. And it only got better.

"Speed, knockdown, you like the knockdown—gives the nervous system a shock," he reiterated. "You want hard and fast. One shot: get them before they get you."

Frank Garcia had just afforded me a complete verbal dissertation as to why the Glock .40 was the best handgun to carry for the purpose of killing another person. I especially liked the "get them before they get you" comment. I thought this exchange would provide a jury of his peers a good idea of where this man's priorities were. It certainly assisted us with connecting him to the murder weapon. While it wasn't definitive proof, it portrayed much about the man and why it would be conceivable he was our shooter. It would serve as the icing on the substantive cake of circumstantial and physical evidence we were gathering and building.

As expected, Garcia grew more impatient with me as I began to press him for more. "I know cases in court. I'm not a stupid ass!" he exclaimed, becoming more animated with his facial and hand gestures. "What I tell you! You're wasting my time here! I wasn't even there. I wasn't even there." His frustration gave way to hostility and a venomous tone that was now directed at me. "I'm not waiting! You either charge me or you let me go or call my lawyer!" he demanded.

"OK," I responded calmly.

"You either charge me—I'm not waiting anymore! I haven't done shit! You either let me go—charge me or let me go!" he demanded a second time. "Fuck it. I've been compliant with you. I answered your crap. I answered all your stuff without getting the Fifth or Sixth [referring to his rights]. I'm not repeating myself."

As he continued to spew more venom at me, Garcia said, "Every criminal got Glocks."

"How did you know there was a Glock at the scene?" I asked pointedly, attempting to keep him off balance. He had just stepped on himself during his emotional tirade when he indicated that a Glock pistol was involved in the shootings.

His countenance changed to worrisome for a split second. "I didn't say there was a Glock at the scene," Garcia answered.

"Well, you said criminals carry Glocks," I said.

"I didn't say that! What are you talking about?" he shot back, becoming angry with me again.

Another baldfaced lie was registered on the recording. He just denied saying something that he obviously said. Garcia tried to rationalize why he said what he said about the Glock, but I eventually moved the conversation to another topic to avoid an argument and shutting him down.

Mug shot of Frank Garcia. *Courtesy of the Monroe County Sheriff's Office.*

"Do you know anybody in Farmington?" I asked.

"No," he said.

"Are you sure?" I asked.

"Positively," he responded.

"Because this number comes back to Farmington," I said, referring to the Glatzes' cellphone number. I then asked Garcia if he had ever been to the Canandaigua area, which is adjacent to the town of Farmington.

"Years ago," he answered. Garcia denied being in Canandaigua, knowing anyone who lived in the area or calling from a phone number there that day. There was no denying that he called his wife from the number while she was in the presence of the police, so he was forced to provide an explanation as to where he made the call from.

Frank Garcia had had enough. After one last rant about how he was being unfairly mistreated, he finally decided to shut his trap and invoke his right to remain silent and retain counsel. Little did Garcia know, despite his vehement denials, he gave us a lot more than he had expected. While he attempted to maintain a reticent posture during the interview, his manic outbursts of egotistical declarations were going to come back to haunt him.

Like so many other unforthcoming suspects I've interviewed over the years, Frank Garcia thought he was smarter than the average mope and tried to talk his way out. Telling the police several lies, all of which contradicted witness testimony and physical evidence, during a recorded interview would prove to be a serious error in judgment. He should have kept his mouth shut from the beginning, but his narcissistic and arrogant personality could not contain itself. He was too compelled to be "the man."

Garcia's clothes, shoes and jewelry were confiscated and secured as evidence. The clothes and shoes would be processed by the Monroe County Public

Crime lab located in downtown Rochester. *Courtesy of Gene Renner.*

Safety Lab for blood, tissue and other serological and trace evidence that could connect him to one or both of the murder scenes. His wedding band would eventually be identified by Mrs. Glatz's daughter to be the same ring they had described to the sheriff detectives as being worn by the man who murdered their parents.

Search warrants were executed on Garcia's vehicle and his residence. Ontario County searched the Glatzes' residence for additional evidence that could connect Garcia to their murders. A piece of notepad paper with my name and phone number was recovered from Garcia's vehicle. It was matched to a notepad at the Glatzes' residence. This confirmed both my suspicion and fear that Garcia was in the process of terrorizing this poor family while I spoke with him on the phone earlier that day.

After he was allowed to use the bathroom under the watchful eye of a uniformed deputy, deprived of all his personal belongings, provided with a loosely fitting beige jail uniform and slip-on canvas footwear, reality must have struck Frank Garcia right between the eyes. He wasn't going anywhere except jail.

As the self-portrayed patriot sat alone in the interview room contemplating what it was going to be like to sit in a prison cell for at least four life sentences and some change for the brutal murders he refused to take responsibility for, we collaborated with detectives from the Ontario County Sheriff's

Office to make sure we could lock him in his rightful place in the New York Department of Corrections. Since Garcia had asked for his attorney, he could not continue the interview without counsel. The interview would be continued at a later time if his lawyer agreed to it, which was highly unlikely.

The Ontario County detectives compelled Garcia to stand in a physical lineup at the Monroe County Jail that was viewed by Mrs. Glatz's children. Other inmates who possessed similar physical characteristics were recruited by Monroe County Jail deputies to voluntarily serve as the other participants in the lineup. After viewing the lineup behind a mirrored glass from an adjacent room, Mrs. Glatz's daughter positively identified Frank Garcia as the person who murdered her mother and stepfather in the sanctity of their home.

After consulting Assistant District Attorney Doug Randall, I drafted a felony complaint against Frank Garcia on behalf of Brockport Village Police officer Steve Misiti. The Major Crimes Unit made it a practice to place the name of a member of the police department we assisted in a major case on the felony complaint as the complainant. This was a form of professional courtesy. Even though we conducted the investigation, identified and caught the killer, it was not our desire to alienate the police officers of a smaller department we were assisting with the perception that we come in and "steal" their thunder and block the limelight that comes along with working high-profile investigations. We even extended this courtesy to our own uniformed members whenever possible. Uniformed officers must perform a thankless and redundant job on a daily basis and deserve some recognition when they assist detectives in a major crime investigation.

Per the felony complaint, Officer Misiti arrested and charged Frank Garcia with two counts of murder in the first degree for the murders of Randall Norman and Mary Silliman and one count of attempted murder in the second degree for shooting Audry Dillon. After he was transported to his arraignment in Brockport Village Court, where he was formally presented with the charges against him, Garcia was incarcerated in the Monroe County Jail in lieu of no bail to await his next court appearance. The Ontario County Sheriff's Office and District Attorney Michael Tantillo chose to arrest and charge Garcia for the Glatz murders and other related crimes on another day. There was no reason to hasten the process since Frank Garcia wasn't going anywhere anytime soon.

Both exhausted and wired, a few of us went out for chicken wings and beers at the late-night hour to decompress and review the day's events. This tradition served as a form of debriefing with each other after an all-hands-on-deck-style call-in. We caught our breath, broke each others' stones and talked about what follow-up work we needed to do in the investigation during the coming days and weeks for the prosecutors, who would be preparing to present the case to a grand jury. After the debriefing ritual ran its course, I would usually go into a vegetative state, allowing everything to slowly dissipate from my mind. Once our stomachs were full and the bill was paid, we exited Jeremiah's Tavern into the dark, bitter cold night and returned to our unmarked police vehicles parked along Monroe Avenue for the trip back to the homes we left nearly twenty four hours earlier. As I drove home in a zombie-like trance, I prayed we get some very much needed sleep before the next job came in.

On the following Tuesday morning, I was in the office of Bob Maldinado, the director of security at Nazareth College, which is located in the upscale township of Pittsford. A retired New York State trooper, Mr. Maldinado had called the sheriff's office to report that Frank Garcia left a verbal message on the voice mail of his college professor and advisor, Linda Janelli, on the early morning of the murders. Maldinado advised that Professor Janelli had been out of town but checked her office voice mail over the weekend and discovered the disturbing message from Garcia.

According to Maldinado, Professor Janelli felt compelled to report the message to the local authorities after hearing about Garcia's reported involvement in the recent murders. Professor Janelli said Garcia's message was left on her voice mail on February 14 at about 5:50 a.m. She gave the security director permission to access her voice mail to listen and record the message from Garcia since she was not returning to Rochester for several more days.

With Maldinado's assistance, I listened to Garcia's message and then recorded it on my pocket-size digital recorder. Garcia's voice was low. He sounded both despondent and apologetic. "Ms. Janelli," he started the message, "I'm sorry I let you down. Another girl said I raped her. I had to take care of business. I'm really sorry." By Garcia's tone of sincerity and the content of his message to Professor Janelli, I concluded that he must have held her in high esteem. I was optimistic that the woman might be able to shed some light on this tragic situation since Garcia's message indicated he had confided in her about his past. Something he refused to disclose or even acknowledge to me during his interview.

Before I left his office, Mr. Maldinado advised that he never received a complaint against Frank Garcia. However, he did have contact with him. Maldinado said Garcia requested to carry his firearm while on campus.

Maldinado said he told Garcia that he was not allowed to possess any type of firearm while on the college property. Garcia reportedly complied with Maldinado's directive, and they remained on friendly terms.

About ten days later, I met with Professor Linda Janelli in her office at Nazareth College. Professor Janelli, a Caucasian, sixty-year-old woman and retired military officer, resided in Buffalo, New York. She made the hour drive to Rochester to fulfill her duties as the director of the geriatric master's program for nursing at Nazareth College. According to Professor Janelli, Frank Garcia was a night-shift supervisor at Wesley Nursing Home on East Avenue in the city of Rochester and held a bachelor's degree in nursing when he applied for the master's program at Nazareth.

Several months later, while attending his first semester of classes, Garcia disclosed that he was having problems at the Wesley. Garcia said someone was falsely accusing him of sexual harassment. Garcia told Professor Janelli he was concerned about his name being "besmirched" in the Rochester health community and being blackballed from working in facilities located in the area. Garcia said he was hiring a lawyer. Professor Janelli said she never learned of the outcome nor did she ask Garcia about it.

Almost a year later, Garcia disclosed to Professor Janelli that he was having similar problems at Lakeside hospital but did not offer specific details of the situation. Professor Janelli said she knew Garcia's wife was expecting another child and his mother was suffering through a serious illness. Despite all these distractions, Professor Janelli said Frank Garcia was a very conscientious, dedicated student and professional nurse who excelled in his clinicals and demonstrated a sincere caring for his elderly patients.

Professor Janelli said she never received a complaint about Garcia from other students, school staff or his clinical preceptors. She recently had asked Garcia to coordinate the Hispanic Wellness Clinic Centro-de-Oro, which is located in the city of Rochester. Janelli said he was well liked and considered to be very dedicated by the staff of the center.

I contacted and met with both of Garcia's nursing preceptors that he worked under while completing his required clinical work in a medical care facility. Both of them had nothing but good things to say about him. They described Garcia to be a professional, attentive and motivated student nurse practitioner. Neither of them ever observed him to act inappropriate toward other medical staff and patients nor did they ever hear him complain about any ongoing turmoil in his life.

Oddly enough, Frank Garcia was a stellar graduate student who performed exemplary in the classroom setting and clinical setting. It was a stark contrast to his workplace persona, where he was described as a manipulative predator of women. He used his authority as a supervisor to capitalize his contact and control of the women who worked with and for him. Looking for weaknesses in their personalities and difficulties in their personal lives, he would manipulate the women who responded to his queries.

Coming up alongside them during their times of need, Garcia purposely placed himself in pivotal positions to influence female co-workers' decision-making processes when negotiating through personal or professional difficulties. Utilizing his authority in the workplace and charismatic personality that was laced with a fair amount of professional intellect and worldly knowledge, Garcia would attempt to seduce those who responded to his attention. If his prey then withdrew once they realized they had been drawn in too deep, Garcia would invoke his authority over them in an attempt to get them back on track.

This is what I believed happened with Mary Silliman and Kim Glatz. We will never know exactly what transpired between them and Frank Garcia, for they are not able to tell their sides. Knowing what I know, I believe Garcia pursued these women in the workplace like a predator. He studied them and identified their vulnerabilities. Once their weaknesses were exposed, both women were no match for this man's manipulative and controlling personality.

How far things went between them and their pursuer would only be a guess. However, both women must have, at some point, come to realize Garcia's true intentions with them and attempted to withdraw from the situation. Kim Glatz even went on the offensive in the legal arena to hold this creep accountable for his actions. Tragically, it cost both of them their lives. Frank Garcia was a man who did not take "no" for an answer once he felt in that squirrelly mind of his that a woman owed him something he rightfully deserved.

I have always held supervisors in the workplace to a high standard. They hold a position of significance in any organization. Their main purpose is to hold employees accountable and empower them to do their jobs effectively. They have daily control over other people's lives, whose livelihoods depend on earning livings to support their families. When bosses lack the necessary people skills to manage the different personalities beneath them, they are ineffective and a detriment to the organization and those individuals they oversee.

When supervisors or managers resort to subversive and dishonest tactics, causing division among the troops, I consider them nothing more than scumbags. These people strive on discord and revel in the divide-and-conquer method of managing others. They have no business being in a management or leadership position. Being nothing more than bullies, they enjoy intimidating people simply because they have the power to. Similar to those individuals who impart domestic violence and verbal abuse on the people they are supposed to support and protect in the home environment, the lowlife supervisors practice a form of emotional terrorism upon those they have control over.

Most of us have worked for, or next to, one of these power mongers at some point in our lives. Their agendas are evil and self-serving. Frank Garcia's actions epitomized this repugnant behavior. Coercing his subordinates into having a sexual relationship with him is about as low as one can go. True to form of this reptile, when Garcia was exposed and sent packing, he displaced blame and sought unwarranted vengeance. Tragically, his form of vengeance was violence.

In the following months we prepared for the grand jury, the suppression hearings where the evidence is challenged by the defendant's lawyers and two high-profile trials. Since Frank Garcia murdered people in two separate counties, we had to prosecute him twice, in Monroe County and Ontario County. That meant several of us from the Monroe County Sheriff's Office had to testify in two separate grand juries, two separate suppression hearings and two separate trials. Anyone in law enforcement who testifies on a regular basis knows this is no easy task.

Where the grand jury is a nonadversarial process and considered a cakewalk for those of us who testify often, the suppression hearings equate to minitrials in front of only the presiding judges prior to the trials. They must rule on whether the police obtained the evidence lawfully and did not violate the defendant's constitutional rights while doing so. Many cases are won or lost at the suppression hearing. If valuable evidence is tossed out, it may force the prosecutor to allow the defendant to take a plea to a much lesser charge or even dismiss the case altogether. If the evidence was held in, then it may motivate the defendant to accept a plea that requires the maximum sentence to avoid the embarrassment of a highly publicized trial.

If the defendant doesn't accept a plea bargain, we must do it all over again in front of a jury at the trial. As I've told the victims and deceased victims' families I've worked with over the years, the United States Constitution was designed to protect the rights of the accused, not expose the whole truth or ensure justice for the victim.

Some people believe violent criminals in our society today don't play by the rules; therefore, they are not entitled to their constitutional rights, especially when the evidence overwhelmingly demonstrates their guilt of committing a horrible crime. I empathize with this sentiment, especially by those who have been victimized by one of these animals. However, law enforcement must always operate by a set standard of rules and not be allowed to deviate from those rules of law when it suits them in order to protect the rights of everyone. None of us know when we (or a loved one) might be wrongfully accused of a crime we did not commit, nor do we expect to. But it does happen.

Testifying at multiple hearings for crimes connected to the same suspect creates a mountain of court transcripts to review and remain familiar with over the months leading up to the trial. While I always tell the truth to the best of my ability when I testify under oath, defense lawyers can have a field day with you on the witness stand if you don't keep your testimony consistent. They will pepper the law enforcement witnesses with questions of detail in an attempt to confuse them about what they have said in past court appearances or written in the reports in an effort to make the witnesses look less than competent or even dishonest. When given the opportunity, some defense lawyers take great pleasure in eviscerating the law enforcement officer offering inconsistent testimony while on the witness stand. Inconsistent testimony does not necessarily equate to perjury but rather lack of preparation.

Preparation is the key. The law enforcement witness must study their reports and transcripts of past court appearances relating to the defendant's crimes in order to keep their answers consistent. Inconsistencies in their testimony could hurt the prosecutor's case. And when one is involved in the prosecution of murders and other major crimes, the last thing desired is to be singled out as the law enforcement witness who caused a mistrial or, worse yet, an undeserved acquittal. The most stress I have ever encountered on this job is the pressure of testifying in a major case. And I have testified in many.

To make our task of testifying even more arduous, when several of us from the Monroe County Sheriff's Office testified in Ontario Court about the Glatz murders, we were not allowed to make any reference to the murders at Lakeside hospital. And when we testified in Monroe County Court about the Lakeside hospital murders, we were not allowed to make any reference to the Glatz murders in Ontario County. This was similar to walking through a landmine field on one leg with one hand tied behind your back. An accidental slip-up or lapse of judgment could cause a mistrial, requiring the judge to order a new trial with a new jury. None of us wanted to be that guy.

For me, being restrained from making references between the two cases made it difficult to testify in a fluent manner. Most of us remember experiences in sequential order. Because we investigated the murders jointly with Ontario County, it made it all the more difficult to separate them in my mind. When I testify in court, I am reciting a chronology of observations and actions relative to an investigation I was assigned to conduct. One observation or action leads in to another and so on. When forced to exclude some of those events, it makes the task of recall more difficult than it already is, requiring me to reflect longer than I normally would before answering a question. Certain answers may sound incomplete—as if I excluded something important—which I did because I was directed to. The jurors, having no clue of what you've been asked to do, can sometimes interpret your responses as contrived or even less than honest.

The forensic exam that was conducted on Garcia's laptop computer showed Garcia already knew about the Lakeside hospital shootings before I made my first contact with him. The examination revealed that Garcia had been viewing news stories about the Lakeside hospital shootings on several of the Rochester news media websites prior to my advising him of Mary Silliman's murder that morning. An innocent man would have told me he had already read about the shootings when I informed him of my purpose for calling him. Feigning surprise, Garcia acted as though it was the first time he heard the news and requested time to get himself together before meeting with me. The computer forensic evidence proved him to be a liar.

As we listened in on the recorded phone calls from jail between Garcia and his pregnant wife, it became clear that he did not possess an ounce of remorse or contrition for what he had done. His draconian demeanor was overbearing and even offensive at times. During their daily conversations, Garcia barked instructions at her about their children and household issues. Understandably, there were times she sounded despondent in regard to the position her womanizing husband had just placed her in.

I truly felt sorry for this woman, who seemed to be a decent and nice person. Her love and devotion toward her undeserving spouse was obvious. However, as the weeks turned into months, Mrs. Garcia grew tired of the unwarranted verbal hostility he was subjecting her to. Her life was now in financial and emotional destitution because of this man's violent and selfish actions. As Garcia realized he was losing his controlling grip over her, he became unnerved and more agitated. I considered Mrs. Garcia and their children secondary victims in this tragedy and smiled to myself when I would overhear her put "Frank" in his place.

During my preparation for the suppression hearing and trial in Ontario County, I met with Mike Tantillo, the Ontario County district attorney.

Known for his no-nonsense attitude when dealing with the criminal element in his county, I found him to be personable and great to work with. The suppression hearing was held in the early part of summer, and the trial was commenced about two months later. Both court proceedings were high-profile media events.

Dressed in a suit and tie, Frank Garcia was in his glory, eating up the media attention and spotlight. It made him a jailhouse hero to many of the young thugs awaiting their own criminal trials. Several of the photographs in the local newspapers captioned him either smiling or laughing with his lawyers while seated in court. It was obvious to me he was enjoying every minute of it. Most defendants would rather sit in court than in a prison or jail cell.

It was very evident to me that Garcia enjoyed knowing his court hearings and trials would be attended by loyal family members of his victims, requiring them to sit through all the long and drawn-out courtroom drama. He took gratification knowing they would be exposed to the horrible details of their loved ones' violent deaths. Garcia's hatred for Kimberly Glatz ran especially deep. Her brutal murder and last moments of suffering and horror were not enough. His perverted revenge toward this woman would not be quenched until he ripped apart her friends' and family's memories of her.

Garcia was hellbent on taking the witness stand. His only motive for testifying was to publicly trash the reputations of both women. It was Garcia's intention to portray both Kimberly Glatz and Mary Silliman as promiscuous women, claiming they had lodged sexual harassment complaints against him only after their personal relationships with him had ended. Both of his lawyers, David Morabito and Joe Damelio, talked him out of it, however.

Frank Garcia's suppression hearing and trial for the Glatz murders were held in the majestic Ontario County Courthouse, which also houses the Ontario County District Attorney's Office. The hulking cream-colored stone building with its large metal-domed roof and massive white pillars sits at the top of Main Street overlooking both the small city of Canandaigua and beautiful Canandaigua Lake, where lakefront property prices challenge that of Lake Tahoe.

As expected, there was a swarm of media at each of Garcia's legal proceedings. Over two decades of working high-profile cases I have learned to get along with members of the press. I recognized they have a job to do and look at them as professionals who have families to support. As a result of showing up at the same crime scenes over the years, I was on a first-name basis with several of them. While waiting for my turn to testify outside

Ontario County Courthouse: the location of Frank Garcia's murder trial in Ontario County. *Courtesy of Gene Renner.*

courtrooms for hours on end more times than I can remember, it was not uncommon for me to become engaged in substantive conversations with several of the reporters and cameramen. If nothing else, it helped the time pass by while I awaited my name to be called by the court deputy.

The topics of discussion would include everything and anything except the case I was to testify about. I particularly enjoyed learning about the journalists' personal backgrounds and families. I believe everyone possesses an interesting story to tell, even members of the media—many of whom were not accustomed to being the object of discussion. This repeated interaction enabled me to cultivate a relationship of mutual respect and fairness that benefited both parties without diminishing the integrity of either.

As I walked into the large courtroom in Ontario County for the first time to testify at Frank Garcia's suppression hearing, I felt like I took a step back in time. The dark wood trim, high ceiling and parade of large portraits that hung on the walls came together for a regal atmosphere. Without an inch to spare, the witness stand was squeezed between Judge Craig Doran's bench, which resembled an oversized ornate desk from the nineteenth century, and the jury box, located to my right. I could have rested my feet up on the rail it was so close.

During the trial later that summer, I felt as though I was sitting on the laps of the jurors in the front row when I testified. The judge had a small brass lamp positioned on the corner of his bench closest to the witness stand. It created a kind of cozy ambiance that I was not accustomed to in the Spartan contemporary courtrooms of Monroe County. The whole setting reminded me of a scene out of *Matlock*, a popular television show about a sage defense lawyer in the South who always prevailed in proving his client's innocence.

When it came time for me to make a positive identification of the defendant in court, I purposely locked eyes with Garcia, pointing my finger at him in a menacing fashion as I described his physical appearance for the court record. I was hoping he could hear my thoughts as we momentarily peered at each other throughout the hearings and trials. I was grieving inside for the families of Christopher and Kimberly Glatz, as they sat in the courtroom listening to my testimony. This arrogant man took great pleasure in retraumatizing these people.

Enjoying the public spotlight, narcissistic criminals like Frank Garcia become cocky and full of themselves when sitting next to their legal advocates in the courtroom. They do every subtle thing possible to intimidate those testifying against them. Menacing stare downs of witnesses is a typical strategy of such defendants.

Many defendants, like Frank Garcia, take great pleasure in revictimizing their victims and other witnesses while their defense lawyer aggressively cross-examines them. While I believe in our constitutional right to confront our accusers and cross-examine them, I've known some defendants' sole purposes to go to trial were so they could terrorize their victims one last time. A plea of guilty would take that opportunity away. This form of legalized courtroom terrorism is common in domestic violence and stalking cases.

Watching a defense lawyer aggressively cross-examine the police witnesses is a defendant's vicarious way of slapping the cops around for locking him up and sending him to prison. With over two decades of court preparation and testifying in major crimes cases, I have taken my fair share of lumps from good, unforgiving defense lawyers. The experiences made me better and prepare harder.

David Morabito, a prominent defense lawyer from Monroe County, was assigned by the judge to defend Garcia since no defense lawyers in Ontario County would accept the case as assigned counsel. Some weren't available and others feared the citizens of the local community would boycott their legal practices if they chose to defend the coldblooded killer. The spectacled Morabito was a good fit for both the defendant and the rural, upscale bedroom community of Canandaigua. Beneath his mild-mannered temperament and polite personality is a savvy lawyer.

Judge Doran subsequently ruled that all the evidence against Garcia, including my recorded interview with him, could be used at trial against him, but he required that any discussion about the Brockport (Monroe County) murders would have to be redacted from the recording and not viewed by the jury. The judge agreed with the defense attorney's argument that evidence and testimony related to the Brockport murders would be prejudicial toward the defendant's right to a fair and impartial trial in Ontario County.

In lieu of the judge's decision, District Attorney Mike Tantillo opted to not use the recording at the trial and limit my testimony to avoid a possible mistrial. I would testify only about what Garcia told me related to his whereabouts the day of the murders and how it contradicted his documented cellphone locations, along with his denials of being anywhere near the Canandaigua and Farmington areas.

When it came time for Heather Glatz to testify at Garcia's trial in Ontario County, everyone sat quietly in restrained anticipation. Other than quiet sobbing and gasps of grief from relatives in the audience, the courtroom was dead silent as the courageous young girl provided the jury her chilling account of what occurred in her home on that cold wintry Saturday morning. I really hated Garcia for putting this child through the agony of having to relive this nightmare in the unforgiving and adversarial environment of a courtroom. However, as she had done on that tragic day, Heather confronted him and sealed his fate. With her riveting testimony serving as her sword, she alone slay the dragon. Mike Tantillo said he could have rested his case after Heather stepped off the witness stand. The remainder of us witnesses that followed her served as nothing more than mere fluff.

The suppression hearing and trial for the Brockport murders were held later that same year in Monroe County. It was nothing more than an act of dreadful redundancy. If Garcia had any bit of human decency and compassion, he would have pleaded guilty. But he doesn't—and he didn't. Already having been sentenced to two life sentences and some change for the Glatzes' murders, one would think he might consider sparing the victims' families further pain. No such luck. Furthermore, the Monroe County trial required survivor Audrey Dillon to relive that horrible morning on the witness stand and be cross-examined by Garcia's defense counsel, Joe Damelio.

During his summation, which was carried live on a local television news station, Joe Damelio took a seat on the witness stand and imitated the way I sat in the chair as he spoke about my testimony to the jury. He described me to be a polished testifier, one who is very comfortable testifying. Labeling me a professional witness, Damelio insinuated that I should not be trusted.

My wife was annoyed by the characterization. I was amused and viewed it as a backhanded compliment. If that's the worst a defense attorney can say about you as a law enforcement witness during a summation, then you've done your job well.

From what I was told by a few people who sat through the entire trial, every one of the sheriff's detectives and crime scene technicians, along with Rochester Police officer Koehn, did an outstanding job testifying in this case. The only reason I can think as to why Joe Damelio, whom I consider to be a very good defense lawyer, singled me out is that I was the only police officer that had any substantive conversation with Frank Garcia. In the end, Garcia was convicted on all counts and subsequently sentenced to two additional life sentences.

After the second trial was finished, I received some additional chilling information about Frank Garcia via a phone call from someone very close to him. According to the confidential source, Garcia had comprised a list of nearly twenty people he wanted to murder as revenge for what he perceived as unjustified terminations from his last two employers. Whether this list was written out or established only in his mind was not shared. However, the caller said it existed, and Garcia was hellbent on fulfilling it. Had he not been stopped, Frank Garcia would have killed several more people that day. And apparently he has openly seethed about how he was bamboozled into meeting with me that afternoon and prevented from achieving his diabolical goal. The source implied that Garcia was mad at me specifically for misleading him and would seek revenge if ever given the chance. To that I say, "Stand in line, Frank."

While Garcia thought he was playing my colleagues and me as fools, we ultimately played him the fool. It was great teamwork that led to the apprehension of this violent criminal. After solving a case such as this one, we (as Major Crimes investigators) rarely walk away with an overabundance of satisfaction. We did what was expected of us. While we took a dangerous murderer off the street, the end result remains an immeasurable loss for the victims, their families and the community.

# EPILOGUE

While it would be easy to focus on the evil aspect of this tragic case, I urge the reader to focus on the courageous, selfless acts of those who sacrificed their lives for others. Frank Garcia isn't worth remembering. He will never

Photo depicts a memorial for the two shooting victims located at the site they were murdered by Frank Garcia. *Courtesy of Gene Renner.*

be eligible for parole, so forget him. To allow his evil acts to preoccupy one's thoughts would be keeping this narcissist's legacy of vengeance alive. And that's just what he wants. The best thing to do to Frank Garcia is to forget he ever existed and deny him the infamy he seeks. Look upon him with indifference.

Rather remember the heroic actions of Randall Norman and Audra Dillon. They came to the aid of Mary Silliman, a woman they didn't even know, as she was being brutally assaulted. Mr. Norman made the ultimate sacrifice, while Audra Dillon sustained life threatening gunshot wounds. Being the only witness, she ultimately provided the police a basic physical description of the shooter and what occurred in the parking lot of Lakeside hospital that early morning.

Focus on the heroic actions of the entire Glatz family. Both parents and children displayed tremendous courage in the face of certain death, as they stood up to a demonic, diabolical madman who violated the precious sanctity of their home. Focus on the valor of Christopher Glatz, who could have escaped harm's way but chose to willingly lay down his life for those he loved.

I'll never understand why God allows humans to commit such senseless, horrible acts of violence against one another. I doubt anyone will ever know the answer to that question on this side of eternity. What I have chosen to remember and focus on about this case is how the aforementioned selfless acts of the victims epitomize agape and goodness that still exist in this darkened world. They did not die in vain.

*Case 2*

# Hate + Revenge = Murder

*The human heart is the most deceitful of all things, and desperately wicked.*
*Who really knows how bad it is.*
*—Jeremiah 17:9*

Monroe County Sheriff's deputy Steve Scott was patrolling the Penfield area when he was dispatched to a domestic dispute on Belvista Drive. The job came in from a third-party caller, so it was unclear as to where the problem was and the circumstances involved. This was not unusual. Confusion and mayhem are common staples in the world of a patrol officer. Deputy Scott asked the dispatcher to perform a callback to the complainant for more information as he responded to the job.

As fate would have it, he was just around the corner from the job and arrived on scene before the dispatcher was able to get back to him. Not knowing what house to respond to, the patrol officer drove slowly with his head on a swivel, looking for any sign of trouble.

As Deputy Scott drove down the small subdivision street of homes built twenty-five years earlier, he was flagged down by a male who was standing at the end of one of the driveways. The man pointed out the house where the reported domestic trouble had occurred and identified the small sedan pulling out of the driveway as that of the ex-husband of the woman who lived there. Not sure as to what he had, Deputy Scott opted not to pursue the vehicle until he investigated further to determine what, if anything, had occurred. His backup had yet to arrive.

There was no obvious sign of trouble as he pulled up in front of the house and exited his patrol car. He cautiously walked up the driveway, keeping his eyes affixed to the front entrance and windows of the residence for any sign of activity or threat. As he approached the front door, Deputy Scott noticed it was ajar. Announcing his presence, he slowly opened the door further to peer inside.

Deputy Scott was unprepared for what he observed. Lying on the floor directly inside the front entrance of the residence was a middle-aged man. Blood was exiting his body from what appeared to be two bullet wounds in his chest. As the cold winter air rushed in through the opened front door, Deputy Scott observed thick vapors of steam stove piping from each of the fresh bullet holes, taking the man's life with it. Concluding the vehicle he had observed leaving the residence upon his arrival was most likely being driven by the suspected shooter, Deputy Scott asked for the air on the primary channel and put out a broadcast of the vehicle's description to the other responding patrols.

Other than having lunch with my father to celebrate his birthday, it had been a typical gray, lackluster day in early January. Nearing the end of our day's tour of duty, my partner, Investigator Thomas Passmore, and I were conducting a follow-up interview at Pittsford Plaza, which is located in the upscale town of Pittsford on the eastside of the county. The twenty-something male subject we were speaking with had reported that he was robbed at gunpoint the week before while performing an evening bank drop of that particular day's receipts for the establishment at which he was employed. We weren't convinced of his truthfulness. In the midst of inviting him downtown for a second interview to discuss our concerns, my portable hand radio crackled.

"We have a confirmed shooting on Belvista Drive in Penfield," the dispatcher broadcasted over the primary channel. His voice was contained despite the urgency of the situation. Competent dispatchers always maintained control of their vocal cords no matter what tragedy was unfolding. Their calm and confident demeanors transcended to the patrol officers in their cars. It set the tone to maintain one's composure.

"601, 10-4. 77," responded the deputy in the 601 car. His voice was filled with intensity as he acknowledged the call and advised he was responding lights and siren by informing the dispatcher he was "Code 77." If a police officer in the Monroe County Sheriff's Office was involved in a motor vehicle accident while driving lights and siren and had not advised the dispatcher that they were "77," it would result in some serious time off. It was one of the countless General Orders police officers of a modern-day police department are required to follow.

All trying to grab the air at the same time to indicate they were Code 77, several other sheriff cars alerted the dispatcher they were en route as well. Investigator Passmore and I looked at one another, reading each other's minds. I loved my job, but when this particular case came in, it was at a time when we were catching new cases every day and couldn't keep up. And that is precisely when the "big ones" usually hit—when you're drowning in work. Something told me that this was going to be one of those cases.

We had planned on working a couple hours overtime that day to clean up what we believed to be a falsely reported robbery and clear the job. However, Investigator Passmore and I knew what was unfolding on channel one of our police radio meant we'd be working into the next morning. This is the life of Major Crimes–homicide detectives. We were the Mop and Glow Guys.

"Mop and Glow" was one of the monikers I had given our unit over the years. We mopped up violence and carnage into neat and shiny arrest packages for the prosecuting attorneys at the Monroe County District Attorney's Office. Joseph Shur, one of the more aggressive prosecutors I have worked with over the years, has said on a number of occasions, "All the assistant DAs in the Violent Felony Bureau used to fight over arrest packages from Passmore and Crough. We knew an arrest package from them equated to a guaranteed guilty verdict."

After Investigator Passmore and I advised our reported robbery victim that we'd get back to him another time, we were snaking through the rush-hour traffic toward the crime scene, which was located in another upscale eastside town north of our current location. There was no need to respond lights and siren since Deputy Scott advised that the suspect had already fled the scene and our victim was deceased. Deputy Scott further advised that the suspect was known.

A broadcast of the suspect and his vehicle was put out over the primary channel. The suspect was identified as *Edward Taylor, the ex-husband of the decedent's wife, who was also an intended victim but had escaped through the back door of the residence to the neighbor's house, where she called 911.

Upon our arrival to the scene, we found things to be unusually serene and minus the unnecessary brass loitering about. A Road Patrol deputy was hanging the police line tape around the front of the house. A couple of sheriff cars were blocking off both ends of the quiet neighborhood street, allowing only residents to return home from work. The road sergeant was at the neighbor's house with another deputy comforting Taylor's ex-wife and attempting to gain more information from her about what had occurred and where Taylor might be heading.

Investigator Norm Thompson, from our Identification-Crime Scene Unit, arrived on scene shortly after Passmore and me to assist us with the crime scene. The three of us entered the house together through the front door. Deputy Scott was in tow to point out what had taken place based on his observations and a brief conversation with Mrs. Joyce Hall, the decedent's wife and Taylor's ex-wife. The winter sun was beginning its early descent for the day, and a winter wind had just kicked up.

As my colleagues and I viewed the carnage, which was mostly confined to the foyer area of the front door, I got my second wind. Apathy was replaced by a renewed sense of purpose as I focused on the bleeding corpse located at our feet. While our task was serious, the three of us maintained our usual lighthearted tone. This is typical of most Major Crimes–homicide detectives. It prevents the tragedy of the situation from strangling our sense of logic and reason.

Working these types of cases isn't for everyone. And I state that respectfully. Dealing with the sights and smells of blood and guts, along with the sadness of unexpected loss resulting from senseless violence, is not for everyone. Sorting through the emotional strife as one seeks the truth can be challenging and emotionally draining. However, it would be difficult to find a better sense of purpose for those of us who have chosen law enforcement as a career.

"Looks like this guy has a pretty good-sized hole in the back of his head," Investigator Thompson pointed out.

"Looks like our shooter wanted to finish him off after the two shots to the chest," I added.

Peter Hall's twisted body was lying in a large pool of blood on the slate floor of the front foyer. The swift-moving, bright-red arterial blood had pushed and swirled its way through the darker, slow-moving unoxygenated blood, forming the once life-bearing fluid into a pinwheel pattern. It appeared the decedent had been shot twice in the chest, and there was a gaping gunshot wound located on the back of his skull.

According to Deputy Scott, Hall was shot while opening the front door for a man, later identified as Edward Taylor, who was holding a shoebox. Deputy Scott said the grinning, silver-haired Taylor calmly pulled a revolver out of the shoebox and fired at least two rounds into Hall's chest, causing Hall to drop. Based on what Mrs. Hall reported, Deputy Scott said Taylor then stepped over Hall as he was gasping for air on the floor and put one round in his head to finish him off. Taylor then began firing at Mrs. Hall as she turned in horror and ran through the adjoining living room to the rear of the house. We observed three bullet holes in the wall of the living room that were spaced apart. The pattern was consistent with someone shooting at a target as it was moving away from them.

Leaving Investigator Thompson to his work of processing the crime scene before the medical examiner carted Mr. Hall's corpse away, Investigator Passmore and I walked to the neighbor's house next door where Mrs. Hall was being attended to. Just as we were entering the residence through the front, I observed the uniformed road sergeant kneeling down beside a middle-aged woman seated in an oversized upholstered chair in the living room. I overheard him say, "He's gone." The woman let out a yelp and slumped back into the chair as she began sobbing uncontrollably. I deduced that the woman must have been our other intended victim, Mrs. Hall. In light of the situation, I chose to allow her time to grieve and be comforted by her caring neighbors and not attempt an interview.

Having just been notified of her husband's death, I knew Mrs. Hall would not be in any condition emotionally to give us a statement any time soon. The sergeant was able to step away with us into the nearby kitchen and whisper that she had positively identified her ex-husband (Ed Taylor) as the shooter and said he chased her through the first floor of the house while shooting at her after she witnessed him shoot her husband in the head as he was lying on the floor. That was all we needed for an arrest. We could secure a sworn statement from Mrs. Hall the following day.

Shortly after Investigator Passmore and I returned to the crime scene, we were advised by one of the command officers loitering outside the house that Taylor had driven to his ex-wife's seventy-five-year-old mother's house and taken her hostage. The elderly woman reportedly lived in the town of Marion, located in Wayne County, which borders the east side of Monroe County. Minutes later, Passmore and I were cleared to respond to the Wayne County scene to assist the local authorities that were already in the process of setting up a perimeter around the residence.

While en route to the hostage situation in Marion, we overheard a familiar voice calling for me over the primary channel of my vehicle's police radio. It was Lieutenant Mike Broida, the commander of the Monroe County Sheriff Hostage Rescue Team (HRT). I was one of the hostage negotiators on the team. After directing me to a secured secondary channel, Lieutenant Broida advised that the SWAT and HRT had been activated to assist with a hostage situation in Wayne County.

Lieutenant Broida said, "Looks like your shooter took his ex-wife's seventy-five-year-old mother hostage at her residence."

"Well, that saves us the hassle of finding him," I said, trying to consider the upside of the mess we had just been served.

Wayne County was a mostly rural county. The Wayne County Sheriff's Office was a smaller department that could only manage to put out little more than a half-dozen cars to cover the entire county. The New York State Police put a few troopers on patrol from their station in Williamson, but for the most part, 911 emergency calls fell mostly to the sheriff's Road Patrol deputies. It was not uncommon for lone deputies to drive an average of thirty miles from one call for service to the next. Many times, their backup was responding from the same distance or even longer. It was not uncommon for these rural lawmen to finish their daily tours of duty with several hundred miles registered on their patrol cars' odometers. They epitomized the term "Sheriff'n." Unlike cops of urban departments, those of us who served on sheriff road patrols quickly learned how to talk to people and defuse deteriorating situations between hotheaded, irrational combatants to avoid getting our butts kicked prior to our backup's arrival.

Because the smaller rural sheriff's offices of the counties that bordered Monroe County, which possesses a population slightly less than one million people, did not have the extensive resources of metropolitan police departments, the Monroe County Sheriff's Office would activate its SWAT and HRT when the smaller departments caught a job that required a specialized response. We supported the town and village police departments in Monroe County with our special teams. All of our special teams, including the K-9 Unit, Bomb Team and Scuba Squad were second to none in New York State when it came to training, equipment and execution.

The weather was now working against us. The temperature had dropped dramatically, icing up the roads. We were driving as fast as we could on very slick roads and through poor visibility created by the horizontal blowing snow. Lieutenant Broida advised me that it would take him longer to get to the scene since he was responding from the west side of our county. He advised that Taylor had been heard firing multiple gunshots while in the house by deputies who were surrounding the house.

When Investigator Passmore and I arrived in the area, we were directed by deputies and state troopers posted on a roadblock to a residence that was located just four houses north of where our murderer was holding his ex-mother-in-law captive. All the houses on the rural road were spaced out. The makeshift command post was set up in the residence of friendly and hospitable people who knew the seventy-five-year-old hostage well. They described her to be a warmhearted woman who possessed a strong will and wasn't easily intimidated. Apparently her deceased husband had been a lawman many years ago. I was advised that her name was Mary.

Once the Monroe County Sheriff's Office SWAT Team had set up its perimeter around the target house, I placed the first phone call into Taylor about 10:30 p.m. I was seated at the residence's dining room table. Investigator Larry Crawford was the secondary negotiator, whose role is to listen in on the conversation, via a set of headphones, and pass along suggestions to the primary negotiator on a notepad when they get stuck or are at a loss for words. Most importantly, the secondary also offers their assessment of the situation and the subject with whom they are interacting. Unlike the primary negotiator, who can get caught up in the negotiation and fall victim to ambition and the fear of failing, the secondary maintains a clear head and remains detached from the emotion and stress the primary negotiator experiences as a result of interacting with either a volatile and/or despondent subject. In reality, the secondary negotiator plays the most important role during the crisis intervention or hostage negotiation.

Lieutenant Broida was standing by, coordinating with the SWAT Team commander, Lieutenant Glenn Greibus, who made it a point to tell us to take our time. My partner in the Major Crimes Unit, Investigator Tom Passmore, was also seated at the table with Larry and me. He acted as our utility person, passing information back and forth between the HRT, SWAT and the command personnel milling about.

After a few rings, an elderly woman answered the phone. It was Mary. Her voice was trembling from fear. I suspected Taylor was either listening from another phone or standing close enough to hear me. Utilizing a calm and steady voice, I attempted to relax and comfort Mary. I reassured her that she was going to be safe. I actually conveyed more confidence than I really possessed, but it is the job of a negotiator to instill hope in what appears to be hopeless circumstances.

To assess the situation further and obtain intelligence for the SWAT commander, I asked the elderly woman a bunch of questions that only required a "yes" or "no" response and learned the following: Mary confirmed that her ex-son-in-law, Edward Taylor, had in fact taken her hostage and was seated in the living room with her. Taylor was pointing a loaded revolver at Mary with the hammer cocked back and listening to her police scanner. She advised that neither of them was injured, and Taylor had been drinking beer since his arrival.

Our SWAT Team was using its own secured radio frequency, preventing Taylor from listening in. The beer drinking concerned me. Taylor reportedly had his revolver's hammer cocked back, placing the trigger in single action mode. The gun could fire accidentally if he sneezed, coughed or jerked his hand the wrong way. Getting himself intoxicated would only heighten the risk of an accidental discharge. It also would make it more difficult to communicate with Taylor.

Taylor refused to get on the line and speak with me. I had Mary ask him several times to take the phone, but he refused. I could hear him in the background. I was concerned that he might become angry with Mary if she continued to pester him, so I engaged her in conversation to keep things calm. Mary was able to advise me that Taylor had been watching the local news broadcasts on television and was aware that Peter Hall was in fact dead. Another bad break, I thought. It always makes the hostage negotiator's job more difficult when the hostage taker is keeping up with the live news broadcasts about himself.

I then made a feeble attempt to get Taylor on the telephone. I instructed Mary to tell him that we suspected Peter Hall had grabbed Taylor around the neck and a struggle ensued, causing Taylor's gun to go off accidentally. I told Mary to tell him that it was conceivable that he didn't mean to shoot Hall. This was not true, but I was attempting to convey some sense of hope to Taylor that all was not lost.

I heard Mary relay the message to Taylor. Her voice was flat, void of any empathy or sympathy. I was afraid Mary's captor would become annoyed with her, but there was no other way to communicate with him until he got on the phone. I overheard Taylor proclaim boldly that the shooting was no accident and that he meant to kill Joyce too, but she got away. He spoke with conviction and sounded agitated. Mary repeated what Taylor said into the phone. This was not good, I thought. This guy was clearly homicidal and possessed no remorse for his murderous behavior. My concern for Mary's safety ratcheted up a few notches. I concentrated on keeping my voice steady and calm so as not to scare her more than she already was.

After some additional conversation to comfort and relax Mary, I instructed her to ask Taylor to take the phone so he could just listen to me. I told her to tell him that he didn't have to talk if he didn't want to. Whispering, I told Mary to convey empathy in her voice when she asked him to take the phone.

"He wants you to take the phone and just listen," I overheard her tell Taylor. "You don't have to talk if you don't want to." Her voice was still flat. To my surprise, I overheard Taylor agree to the request and being handed the phone.

"Hello," said Taylor. There was no emotion.

"Hello, Ed," I said. "This is Patrick Crough from the Monroe County Sheriff's Office. Thanks for taking the phone." In an attempt to defuse his hostility and make him more comfortable with talking to me, I added, "Let me assure you that you're in total control this situation. Nobody is going to do anything without your approval."

"That's good," he responded in a stern voice.

"Are you OK?" I asked

"I'm great," he answered, his voice sounded upbeat.

"Do you need anything?"

"Nope."

I purposely didn't ask about Mary. Since I had talked to her, I knew she was OK other than being terrified. I wanted Taylor to believe that I was concerned about him and him only. Verbalizing concern for the hostage places too much value on them to the hostage taker. And it would only confirm the obvious: that the negotiator cares more about the hostage than the hostage taker. Generally, most hostage takers in domestic violence situations are looking for both understanding and sympathy relative to their causes. Favoritism toward the hostages could inhibit any kind of rapport building and prevent the negotiator from earning the hostage takers' trust.

Second, the hostage taker will ultimately use the hostages against the negotiator if he feels their well-being is more important than his to the negotiator. I prefer to convey my full attention and support to the hostage taker and minimize the role of his hostages. In fact, if negotiations go in the right direction, I usually refer to hostages as an inconvenience and potential liability to the hostage taker's cause. I will propose that he let me take them off his hands as a token of good faith while we work toward "his goal."

One doesn't say "no" or make ultimatums to a hostage taker, especially when someone else's life is hanging in the balance. In hostage situations that stem from domestic violence, the hostage taker is in a highly emotional state, bent on some form of vengeance. Their initial demands usually involve bringing a third party to them so they can kill that person before they end their standoff. Instead of saying "no" to an unreasonable demand such as this, I prefer to "suggest" that we consider other options to resolve the situation. I let them know that I am sympathetic to their feelings and many times will agree with their desired outcome. However, in time, I make it clear that I am unable to assist them with achieving something that the law and "government policy" won't permit, such as the swapping of one hostage for another.

Again, I suggested to Ed that the shooting of Mr. Hall was a horrible accident as a result of a supposed struggle that I knew did not take place. And, again, it turned out to be a futile attempt to downplay what we all knew was an intentional murder.

"It wasn't an accident," Taylor said, his voice was firm. "I would have killed Joyce, too, but she got away."

"So you intended to kill them both?" I asked.

"Yes." He said. I was not surprised by his response. Knowing the answer to my next question, I asked Taylor, "How do you feel now?"

"I feel great!" he said, happily. "I have my self-respect back."

I leaned back in my chair and stared at the ceiling. "Were you drinking before shooting your ex-wife's husband?"

"Nope," he answered, "I hadn't had a drink in months. Although, I did raid Mary's refrigerator when I got here. Had a few beers to calm my nerves."

"You an alcoholic?" I asked

"Been in recovery since my thirty-day rehab two years ago," he said.

I sipped a hot cup of black coffee that had just been handed to me by Lieutenant Broida. The cardboard cup warmed my hands. I still had on my long, black cashmere wool overcoat. There was a draft of bitter cold air blowing through the small ranch-style home every time one of the uniformed command officers and support staff exited or entered through the front door.

The temperature outdoors was near zero. The high winds placed the wind chill temperature near twenty below. I thought about the SWAT officers on the inner perimeter and regular uniformed personnel on the outer perimeter. They were exposed to the arctic elements for God knows how long, and here I was, annoyed by a draft in a much warmer environment.

During our joint training sessions, I often joked that the HRT was equivalent to the varsity chess team, while the military-clothed and equipped SWAT Team was equivalent to the varsity football team. Unless we were conducting a "face-to-face" negotiation from around the corner of a doorway or behind a bullet shield, hostage negotiators usually conducted their business over the telephone while seated comfortably in a safe and controlled environment.

"Why this, Ed?" I asked, referring to the murder. My voice was low and steady.

"Do you know what 'cuckold' means?"

"Cuckold?" I repeated.

"Yeah, cuckold."

"No."

"Then look it up and call me back," Ed said in an authoritative voice. He was in control and enjoying every moment of it.

"Ed, I don't have a dictionary on hand right now. Why don't you educate me," I said, hoping he wouldn't get pissed at me and hang up.

The line was silent for a long pause and then he said, "Cuckold means a man whose wife is unfaithful." His voice was tight.

"Your ex-wife was unfaithful to you?"

"Since she took off her wedding ring eight years ago." His voice sounded angry now.

"That must have hurt you very deeply," I said, trying to convey sincere concern.

"Fucking right, it did. Now it's payback time," he exclaimed.

"How so?"

"You want the old lady to live?" referring to his hostage.

"I want everyone to come out of this alive, Ed," I said. I closed my eyes and exhaled quietly to keep my voice level. Investigators Crawford and Passmore were both listening on headphones connected to the portable Hostage Rescue Phone console as they sat at the table next to me. Both of them were staring at the table, concentrating on Taylor's responses.

"Then bring that whore here so I can tell to her in person that she's nothing but a fucking whore," he demanded.

"That's it? Anything else, Ed?" I asked

"Nope. It's the next best thing since I didn't get to kill her," he said. His voice was calmer. I think he was expecting me to balk at his demand. His tone softened when I didn't flinch. I knew we'd never allow him to speak to his ex-wife in person, but I wasn't going to say "no" to any of his requests this early in the negotiation. The rapport-building process still had to run its course.

My mission right now was to listen and allow Ed Taylor the opportunity to vent his emotions. There was nothing I could say that would help the situation. In fact, my words, while well intended, would only make matters worse. This guy was homicidal and, most likely, suicidal. He had nothing to lose, and there was nothing I was going to say that would make the situation any better for him. I just wanted to keep him talking and venting his emotions at me and not his hostage. The less I said, the less likely it was that I would provoke him and escalate his anger. I believe there is a reason most of us were born with two ears and one mouth.

An hour into our discussion, Ed continued to vent about his ex-wife's past transgressions and demand that she be brought to the house so he could confront her in person. "I know what you're doing with this stall tactic bullshit, Patrick," he hissed. "Get that bitch here now. Until you do that, we've got nothing to talk about!"

I concluded that it was time to start the negotiation process. "I passed along your demand to the command in the form of a note a while ago, Ed. They won't allow her to come near you."

"Then let me talk to someone in charge," he demanded. I knew he would say that. It was time for honesty.

"Frankly, I can't disagree with them, Ed. You did try to kill her."

"I told you I did."

"I know. How about we work out another option?" I stood up to stretch my back and legs.

"I can't think of one. I want to talk to Joyce in person."

"I know, Ed," I said, searching for the appropriate words to follow up with. "I need a little time to see what I can do about this," I reassured him. "Why don't you think about a possible alternative solution just in case I can't get Joyce to the scene. I'm going to do everything I can, Ed. Just use this time to think about a possible alternative. Work with me—please." I did not want our murderer-hostage taker to believe that I had totally discounted his desire to call his ex-wife a whore in person. For now, I wanted him to believe it was a demand that I would "attempt" to meet—in order to save Mary.

"Call me back in an hour, Patrick," he said. I sensed a hint of empathy in his voice. For whatever reason, he seemed to understand the difficult spot I was in as a negotiator. I believe that he knew his demand would be a difficult one to achieve. How hard he would press it was anyone's guess. But we had a glimmer of hope for the time being. I think Ed felt we were working together. By the grace of God I had not yet pissed him off. But we still had a long way to go.

"I don't need that much time, Ed. Can I call you back in half an hour?" I did not want a full hour to pass. I just needed time to discuss the situation with my colleagues and Lieutenant Broida. The SWAT commander, Lieutenant Glen Greibus, would be consulted as well.

"That's fine, Patrick," he answered and then hung up.

Ed Taylor was making it a point to call me by my first name. It demonstrated we had developed a personal rapport with each other despite our polarized positions. Based on our discussion up until that point, I determined that Taylor did not dislike the police. This was usually a difficult hurdle to overcome since most hostile subjects we deal with as hostage negotiators or crisis intervention specialists have had negative contacts with the police in their pasts and hate everyone in law enforcement. Taylor did not present us with that challenge. Now it was our mission to keep it that way.

I consumed a couple of pieces of cold pizza and room-temperature soda that had been delivered to our makeshift command post as I consulted Investigator Crawford and Lieutenant Broida about our negotiation strategy. My goal was to keep our hostage taker talking and get him to change his mind regarding his demand that he speak to his ex-wife (in person) before surrendering.

I called Ed back after the half hour elapsed. "Did you come up with an alternative plan, Ed?" I asked.

"How about we switch," he said, "I give you Mary, and you give me Joyce."

"We can't switch hostages, Ed," I answered. "They wouldn't even allow me to take Mary's place."

"I wouldn't want to switch for you, Patrick. I'm not upset with you." This statement indicated to me he had other intentions with Joyce other than to hear her confession of infidelity in person. I suspected he wanted to kill Joyce and then himself. As I had mentioned earlier, this was a common objective of hostage takers in incidents related to domestic violence.

"I'm glad you're not mad at me, Ed," I said. "Aside from cheating on you, what else did Joyce do to you?"

Ed accused Joyce of poisoning their children's minds and hearts against him over the years. He said they had abandoned him because of it. Ed said he recently received a letter in the mail that was meant for Joyce and had been mistakenly forwarded to him. That's when he learned of her new address on Belvista Drive and her new husband.

"I never knew she had taken a new man until just recently," Ed said.

"Did you ever meet the guy?" I asked

"Nope. Not until I put a bullet in his head," he said proudly. "Can you believe that bitch was still taking me back to court for more money after marrying this asshole?"

"Why'd you shoot him?"

"Why not?" he said coldly. "That fucker supported Joyce trying to bleed me for more money, and I know for a fact he was fucking her when we were still married." Hatred oozed from his voice.

"Payback time?" I asked, trying to sum up what he told me.

"Yes," he responded. "I wanted to take away her happiness, make things even with him for breaking up my marriage."

"I completely understand your reasoning, Ed. I can't support what you did [officially], but I understand how they drove you to this," I said, trying to maintain a realistic tone of empathy that fell short of patronizing.

"Thank you, Patrick."

I wanted Ed to know I understood where he was coming from without sounding like a phony. While I would never support murderous actions, I have no problem telling a hostage taker or murder suspect that I am sympathetic to their situation and understand how this tragic result is the victim's, or intended victim's, fault and not theirs. Believe it or not, the majority of these people are looking for someone to see it their way.

However, if these individuals think you are not being genuine with your comments and just trying to set them up, such statements could backfire. It is paramount that the hostage negotiator or interrogator not go overboard and come off as though they are patronizing the hostage taker or murder suspect when utilizing a strategy that includes sympathy and empathy. While these people are irrational in their thinking and actions, they are not stupid.

Taylor then told me he had another idea. He said to have Joyce go on live television and confess to being a whore and committing adultery to the entire community on local television. Taylor said after he viewed her confession on the television that he would release Mary. I agreed to pass his idea on to the brass and thanked him for working with me. I doubted any of the media outlets would participate, nor did I believe Joyce would be in any condition, emotionally, to execute such an undertaking, provided she even agreed to bare all her alleged marital transgressions on local television. We agreed to take a "piss break" and allow me time to follow up on his request. I told Taylor I'd call him back in twenty minutes.

As I suspected, the local television stations refused to be used in the negotiations. And Lieutenant Broida confirmed that Joyce was in no condition to fulfill such a request. Understandably, she was too traumatized and had been sedated. I called Taylor back and gave him the bad news. He wasn't happy and became agitated. I blamed the television stations, telling him they did not want to assume any legal liability.

Grasping for words to calm him down, I told Taylor that we had to work together to come up with an alternative solution to his liking. My head was spinning for ideas. After some additional discussion, I suggested that we have Joyce confess to her adulterous ways on an audiotape. I told Taylor the tape would be considered evidence and have to be played at his trial in court. I told Taylor the media would be there to listen to the tape and hear her confession. I assured Taylor the content would then be shared with the public by the media and ultimately accomplish his goal of publicly humiliating her. He was silent for a moment.

"Let's do it," he said, "but if Joyce doesn't sound like she means what she's saying, I'm going to shoot her mother. I want her to say she is a whore and this is all her fault, or Mary's dead."

"OK, Ed. Please keep in mind, she's severely traumatized and heavily medicated," I answered.

"Then sober her up. If I think she is saying this just to save her mother, Mary gets a bullet in the brain," he warned. I could hear the conviction in his voice and knew he was serious. He already put a bullet in the brain of Joyce's husband.

"OK, Ed. That may take some time." I was skeptical as to whether Joyce was capable of pulling this off.

"We've got plenty of food and drink to last a few days in this place. Take all the time you need," he said.

Then, as if someone flipped a switch, Taylor's mood turned dark. "But keep in mind, Patrick. If I think I'm going to fall asleep, I'll shoot Mary in the legs and make her suffer like her daughter made me suffer."

Where in the hell did that come from, I thought to myself. I looked over at Investigator Crawford, who was listening in. He gave me a look that portrayed the same thought. Within the blink of an eye, this guy went from conveying a sense of reason and patience to placing us under an incalculable time constraint bolstered by a very real threat.

Just when we think we have a good rapport with the hostage taker and are making progress, they throw you a curveball that smacks you in the face, leaving a sting of uncertainty.

Such setbacks can put the hostage negotiators back on their heels and knock the confidence out of them if they don't maintain a proper perspective throughout the negotiation. Not keeping our expectations and emotions in check can cause us to respond inappropriately. Conveying anger or disappointment with the hostage takers when they make threats or renege on agreements that were difficult to attain in the first place could prove to be a catastrophic mistake. Hostage negotiators need to keep their egos in check and not operate as if they are in competition with the hostage takers, trying to defeat them by obvious manipulation. If the hostage takers believe your only goal is to convince them to surrender and not assist them with their problems, the situation will reverse very quickly. You will have lost all credibility in their eyes as a negotiator and more than likely never regain it. The hostage takers already know that the police want them to release the hostages and surrender. That's why it is paramount to focus on assisting them with their problems and maintaining their dignity and self-respect. If the hostage taker feels the negotiator is being genuine and truthful, trust will eventually follow in most situations. Once trust is achieved, then it is just a matter of time until a voluntary surrender is accomplished.

After taking a deep breath and exhaling it slowly, I responded to Taylor's threat in a voice that conveyed as much empathy as I could muster.

"I understand, Ed. I am going to do everything in my power to get this done as quickly as possible."

"I don't want to hurt Mary. I've got nothing against her. But I will kill her and then myself to get back at Joyce," he said.

"I understand, Ed," I said again. "Do you have coffee in the house? I need you to stay awake."

"Yeah, we'll put some on," he answered.

"Maybe ease up on the beer if you haven't already. That can make you sleepy," I said, utilizing a voice that expressed both subservience and concern.

"I already have, Patrick."

"Thank you, Ed. I'll get back to you as soon as we have something for you to listen to."

I terminated the call. He seemed to be in a better place for the time being.

Lieutenant Broida and Road Patrol sergeant Glen Maid drove to where Joyce was anxiously waiting out the hostage crisis, surrounded by friends and her children. After they updated her as to how the negations were going, they put Joyce on the telephone with me. In a sympathetic voice, I advised the distraught woman of what her ex-husband had been demanding and was now willing to accept. Joyce told me she would make the audiotape of her admitting to being a whore and shouldering the blame for what had occurred earlier that evening at her residence.

This poor woman's world had been destroyed by the selfish and violent acts of this monster the night before and now she was being forced to kowtow to him. As if it wasn't bad enough that she had to put up with his drunken and abusive ways most of her adult life and raise a family in such circumstances, now she had to deal with the tragic loss of her current husband and the possibility of losing her beloved mother. Worse yet, this nightmare was unfolding years after she had escaped Ed Taylor's wake of destruction that he nearly drowned her in for so many years.

I apologized up and down to Joyce as I advised her on what she had to say on the audiotape. I kept telling her that I believed her efforts would save her mother. I was more hopeful than confident. Amazingly, Joyce did not hesitate to say and do what it took to secure her mother's safety. In a voice cracking with emotion, Joyce Hall said what her ex-husband demanded that she say about herself and her alleged indiscretions. Using the HRT cassette recorder, Lieutenant Broida taped Joyce's monologue and then delivered it to the command post.

I called Ed Taylor back. While holding the phone receiver next to the cassette player's speaker, I played the audiotape for him. When the tape was finished, I put the phone back to my ear.

"Not good enough," he said. His voice was void of any emotion.

My heart sunk. "How so?" I asked, trying to keep my anger and frustration from coming through.

"She needs to add how long she's known Peter Hall and when they were married," he demanded.

"OK, Ed. I don't know if she can pull it off. She's pretty messed up. Didn't you hear it in her voice?"

"Fuck her. Then Mary gets a bullet in the brain." I heard the anger and hatred in his voice again.

"I have your word you'll end this if I can get Joyce to talk again?"

"Just get her to say it, Patrick," he ordered. "And she better sound like she means it."

"OK, Ed."

With the assistance of Lieutenant Broida, we got Joyce back on the telephone. I spoke to her again from the command post and advised her of what Ed wanted her to say. Very frightened for her mother's safety, Joyce said she was willing to do whatever it took to assist us in rescuing her mother. As I held the phone's receiver to the cassette recorder, Joyce repeated exactly what her ex-husband demanded. She sobbed throughout the whole second message. Joyce even added, for a second time, that she was to blame for everything that had occurred.

After rewinding the tape, I called Ed Taylor back and played the second portion for him. He was silent for a moment.

"We all set?" I asked. "I've got a bunch of frozen cops in subzero wind out there, Ed," I reminded him. I knew he didn't have any quarrel with the police. During our negotiations, Taylor had mentioned that he felt bad for the officers who were forced to stand out in the cold while we talked on the telephone. Ed tried to convince me to release the officers from their positions on the perimeter so they could get warm, promising he would not attempt to leave the house. I told him that wasn't possible but appreciated the offer and concern.

Taylor finally responded: "OK, Patrick. How do we do this?"

While I was elated that we turned the corner and Taylor was ready to surrender, orchestrating the release of a hostage and safe surrender of a hostage taker without it backfiring was no easy task. If it isn't executed with unlimited patience and the right amount of assertiveness, it can blow up the bridge of trust that was painstakingly built by the negotiator and ultimately set negotiations back for hours.

A common stumbling block to this part of the negotiation can occur over how and where the hostage taker exits the structure they're holed up in. The SWAT Team usually tells the negotiator what door to instruct the hostage taker to leave the house because it provides them the appropriate cover. However, many times the hostage taker is hellbent on walking out another door and won't give in to what the SWAT Team wants him to do. Everyone is exhausted, spent and can see the end is in their grasp. Everyone's emotions are taught and prickly, and now the bastard won't cooperate and just walk out the door the SWAT Team wants so no one gets hurt. It is easy for the negotiator to become impatient and lose their composure at this stage, but they need to hold it together more than ever.

The surrender, more than not, will be the most stressful part of the negotiation for the hostage negotiator. Getting everyone out safely is paramount and rests squarely on their shoulders. Getting ugly with either the hostage taker or the SWAT Team because neither side will give in to the other is not advisable and should be avoided. It is the negotiator's role to remain calm and in control. That's why they are the negotiator—it's their job to get everyone on the same page without sacrificing the safety of fellow officers.

I kindly instructed Taylor to unload his .38-caliber revolver. I asked him if he had any other weapons in the house. He told me he didn't. I then instructed him to have Mary put on her coat and place his empty revolver in her coat pocket.

Keeping Taylor on the phone and cooperative while the SWAT Team placed themselves in position outside the front door to receive the hostage felt like an eternity but took only a couple of minutes. On the SWAT commander's cue, I instructed the hostage taker to allow Mary to walk out the front door alone and for him to remain on the telephone with me. Once Mary was removed safely away from the house, I directed Taylor to walk out the front door with his hands up and wait for instruction from the officers outside.

Ed Taylor was taken into custody at approximately 1:59 a.m. With our seventy-five-year-old female hostage safe and in good health and our murderer–hostage taker in custody and no longer a threat, the standoff was officially over. However, the murder investigation continued.

While everyone was packing up and going to their warm homes, Investigator Passmore and I still had a long night ahead of us. Ed Taylor was turned over to a Road Patrol deputy by the SWAT Team that took him into custody after he was thoroughly searched for weapons and contraband. The Wayne County Sheriff's Office agreed to allow Monroe County to take the lead since we were investigating a murder and attempted murder to which Taylor made verbal admissions during the standoff. Wayne County officials would eventually indict him on a list of serious charges connected to the kidnapping and unlawful imprisonment of Joyce Hall's mother.

The weather had turned progressively worse, making our already long ride back to downtown Rochester twice as long. The temperatures were in the subzero range, leaving the roads a sheet of ice. Road salt didn't work in this type of weather. The blowing snow made visibility out of our ice-crusted windshield nearly impossible. The interior of our unmarked police car didn't start to get warm until we crossed the city line. I was exhausted and emotionally drained from the negotiations with Taylor and could hardly keep my eyes open. Just as my body was finally warming up, we arrived at the Monroe County Public Safety Building, otherwise known as the PSB or HQ.

Monroe County Public Safety Building. *Courtesy of Gene Renner.*

I was thankful that Ed Taylor was talked out and decided to invoke his right to an attorney before talking with us about the murder. We already had his verbal confession. Our conversation with him was light and upbeat. I thanked him several times for surrendering peacefully and sparing Mary's life.

As a hostage negotiator, you should always maintain a rapport with the hostage taker, even after the event is over. One never knows if you or someone else may have to talk him out of a bad situation again. If you blow up the bridge you worked so hard to build with him during the negotiations, it could prove to be disastrous the next time the guy takes a hostage. Unfortunately, we have frequent flyers in this business, so it is good policy to always thank the hostage taker for doing the right thing and follow through with whatever promises you may have made him. I rarely promise anything I can't deliver. There are exceptions to this rule, but they should be avoided at all costs.

Investigator Passmore and I prepared the felony complaint and associated paperwork for Taylor's arraignment while Taylor patiently sat in the interview room next to our office. In Monroe County, we write our own felony complaints, arrest warrants, search warrants and wiretap affidavits. Like most of my colleagues, I've typed many of these documents while half asleep in the middle of the night. And this was long before computers sat on top of our desks. Now I couldn't even imagine not doing them on a computer. Once the paperwork was completed via our IBM typewriters, we called the Penfield town judge.

Hall of Justice. *Courtesy of Gene Renner.*

Like most counties in New York State, Monroe County Sheriff's deputies and New York State troopers are required to arraign their prisoners in Monroe County before a town justice if incarceration is required. That means we must contact one of the town justices of the town where the crime was committed during all hours of the day or night and request their presence at the respective courthouse. This is a huge headache, especially after a long day and night. Some town judges answer their phones and respond to the court in a professional manner. And some judges are nothing more than arrogant political hacks who have no business wearing black robes and sitting on the bench. They are usually the ones who don't answer their phones and then give us weak excuses when they do. If a town judge doesn't answer the phone or refuses to come out, then you have to wait until they decide to respond.

Luckily, on this horrible, late winter night, we didn't have to contend with a cantankerous idiot magistrate. The judge on call that night was one of the professionals who I both admired and respected. Knowing our routine, the local media kept a vigil at the court, awaiting our arrival to catch the "perp walk" to and fro the court for the early morning news. As expected, Ed Taylor was remanded to the Monroe County Jail without bail. The local newspaper featured a large photo of Investigator Passmore and me in our long coats escorting Taylor out of the building that housed Penfield Town Court. Taylor sported a grin on his face. My youthful partner's eyes were half open, but he looked remarkably well, as he always did. I had dark circles under my eyes and looked like a walking corpse.

## Months Later

Ed Taylor hired a high-profile defense lawyer named Tony Leonardo. The tall, square-shouldered Leonardo was always impeccably dressed in $2,000 suits and commanded a courtroom when he stepped inside the bar. His olive complexion, shiny silver hair that was always cut short and perfectly combed in place and gold-rimmed glasses accented a handsome face that most women could not resist admiring. And he knew it.

Based on what I knew about Leonardo, I suspected Taylor had to put down a $25,000 retainer before the lawyer would even consider taking his case. Lawyers know that when someone's long-term freedom and liberty weighs in the balance of Lady Justice, they will spend their life savings, and the life savings of others, to keep their precious freedom.

Understandably, private defense lawyers capitalize on these difficult circumstances. One man's tragedy or loss is another's opportunity. Some lawyers will work feverishly day and night to defend their clients, racking up the billable hours against the big retainer, while others will file a few standard motions in court and then plead their clients guilty in the end for the same exorbitant fee.

Leonardo filed the standard legal motion on behalf of his client to have the statements Ed Taylor made to me during the hostage incident in Wayne County thrown out and not allow the prosecution to use the admissions against Taylor at his trial. The statements consisted of his candid admissions to the intentional murder of Peter Hall and intentional attempted murder of his ex-wife, Joyce Hall. Leonardo contended that I should have advised Taylor of his Miranda warnings before I began speaking with him on the phone that night because the SWAT Team had surrounded the house and would have prevented Taylor from leaving if he chose to. Leonardo argued that these circumstances were equivalent to Taylor being in police custody, thereby requiring that he be advised of his rights before speaking with the police.

Obviously, the prosecution saw it differently and believed the police were not obligated to advise Taylor of his Miranda warnings. The prosecution's response to Leonardo's motion argued that Taylor was not in police custody when he spoke to me but was armed with a loaded handgun and holding a hostage while holed up in a house, shortly after he already murdered someone and attempted to murder a second person.

While the SWAT Team's presence outside the house may have prevented Taylor from leaving the scene, the police did not have control of him or his movements inside the residence nor was there any guarantee that Taylor would not be able to go mobile with his hostage if he chose to leave. When a hostage taker decides to leave a location and uses a hostage as a bullet shield, any number of outcomes can occur.

Additionally, the prosecution appropriately argued that these circumstances also fell within the purview of the public safety exception rule to the Miranda rule. This exception allows for the police to question subjects who are in police custody (without advising them of their rights) when it is their intent to neutralize a volatile situation confronting them and not elicit evidence against the subject they are questioning. Trying to peacefully resolve a hostage situation fits the public safety exception rule.

As expected, the judge granted Ed Taylor a suppression hearing, also known as a "Huntley Hearing" in New York State, to argue his motion and hear my testimony firsthand regarding the facts of the hostage negotiations. This would also provide Leonardo an opportunity to challenge the veracity of my testimony and expose potential inconsistencies via an aggressive cross-examination.

Pretrial suppression hearings usually end up being dogfights in the courtroom. These hearings will test the law enforcement officer's metal as a witness. This is because many judges will allow the defense lawyers to be heavy-handed during their cross-examination of the police witness in their attempts to discredit them and the evidence they are introducing against their clients. This usually makes for a long and difficult day in court for the police witnesses, especially detectives who investigate major crimes and homicides on a regular basis.

It was frustrating for me at times when I knew the judge was allowing the defense lawyer to pursue a line of questioning that was way off the radar, unrelated to the issues of the hearing. That's why it is vital the law enforcement witnesses be well prepared to testify and ready for anything when they take the witness stand. This is especially true for major case detectives, for your reputation as a police witness will follow you throughout your career.

As a professional law enforcement witness who has testified in countless suppression hearings and preliminary hearings, I understand the judges' reasoning for allowing the defense lawyers free rein during this part of the court process. If the court record shows the defense lawyer was afforded every opportunity to aggressively cross-examine the police witness, with hardly any restraint from the judge, the higher courts are less likely to overrule the trial judge if they decide in favor of the prosecution and allow them to use all or some of the evidence against the defendant at their trial.

Trial judges don't like being overruled by the judges in the appellate courts. To avoid this, they tend to be liberal toward the defense lawyers during the contentious suppression hearings, affording them every opportunity possible to challenge the evidence being presented against their clients. A detective can be a star in the interview-interrogation room, but if their performance on the witness stand is lacking, their professional reputation will suffer significantly. One need only to speak with both prosecuting and defense lawyers in their legal community about the major case detectives they work with or against on a frequent basis. I have no doubt their opinions will be based upon those detectives' courtroom performances as police witnesses and nothing else. If detectives can't do what it takes in the courtroom to secure convictions, then they'll never be considered to be the "whole package."

The prosecuting attorney I was working with on this case was Assistant District Attorney Mike Green, who ascended to the first assistant position and was later elected the Monroe County district attorney after the retirement of then district attorney Howard Relin. Mike and I attended the same all-boys Catholic high school, McQuaid Jesuit High, where he was an accomplished wrestler. Slim and wiry with slicked-back hair, Mike's competitive nature on the wrestling mat carried over to the courtroom. As a result, the up-and-coming prosecutor was experiencing great success in the Violent Crimes Bureau of the Monroe County District Attorney's Office.

I enjoyed prosecuting cases with Mike Green because he always was prepared and made sure I was as well. After several prep sessions and nights of studying the case file, including my report, I testified at the Huntley Hearing. My direct testimony went in smoothly and clean. When one testifies on a frequently basis, they become familiar with the different styles of questioning executed by prosecuting attorneys. Some are ill prepared and just plain suck, leaving you virtually naked to defend yourself while sitting on the witness stand. And some prepare well but then go off on tangents they never advised you of, leaving you confused and guessing as to what they are looking for.

Mike Green is one of those several prosecutors I've worked with over the years who not only prepares well, he also executes his strategy in the courtroom exactly the way he prepared you. From a practitioner's standpoint, these prosecutors operate on a different (higher) level than many of their colleagues.

Tony Leonardo's cross-examination of me was more spectacle than substance. He was bombastic and animated, as he waved his long arms around, pacing the courtroom. At times he would lean on the railing next to the witness stand and peer at me as he awaited my answer. Leonardo purposely raised his voice every time he said my name or referred to me as "detective." I fought to keep a straight face as he tried to rattle me and get under my skin with redundant questions that challenged both my competence and veracity. His style was pure Hollywood: entertaining but mostly ineffective. A clever public defender with a more reserved and cerebral approach would have provided more of a challenge.

The judge agreed with the prosecution's arguments on both fronts and allowed the defendant's statements to be presented as evidence against him at trial. The judge's written decision stated in sum and substance that Taylor was not in police custody at the time. The judge agreed that these circumstances did not constitute police custody since the police did not have physical control of Taylor; therefore, Miranda warnings were not required.

The judge also concluded that this incident fell within the purview of the public safety exception to the Miranda rule, which is recognized by the *United States Supreme Court in New York v. Quarles.*

# Hate + Revenge = Murder

It was clear to the judge that my intent while speaking with Ed Taylor during the hostage standoff was to encourage a peaceful resolution to the crisis and save the hostage—not to elicit information about the fatal shooting—and concluded that Taylor's statements were not the product of police interrogation.

Sometime after the judge's decision was rendered, Ed Taylor shuffled into court, chained and shackled, and pleaded guilty to the murder and related charges, including those stemming from the standoff and kidnapping in Wayne County. He was sentenced to life in prison and never heard from again. Understandably, Taylor's children had nothing to do with him as a result of this selfish and violent act. He died years later a lonely man while serving his debt to society in prison.

I had contact with Joyce and her children periodically during the years following this case. We shopped in the same supermarket and frequented some of the same restaurants. They are nice people and always expressed their gratitude for my part in securing the safety of their mother and grandmother, Mary, who eventually passed away several years later. During one of those reunions in an aisle of the supermarket, I reminded Joyce that she also courageously played an important role in getting her mother out safely.

Admitting to transgressions she never committed on the audiotape that her ex-husband demanded shortly after murdering her second husband played a monumental part in resolving the hostage crisis peacefully. The tape was never played in court since Ed Taylor never went to trial. I am grateful that Joyce was never required to testify in what would have been a high-profile trial about this real-life nightmare she and her family were forced to endure. It's punishment enough that they have been forced to live with this tragic memory and substantial loss. My thoughts and prayers remain with them.

*Case 3*

# Spawn of Satan

*Certainly there is no hunting like the hunting of man and those who have hunted armed men long enough and liked it, never really care for anything else thereafter.*
—*Ernest Hemingway,* "On the Blue Water," Esquire, *April 1936*

During the winter and spring of 1992, several women in the greater Rochester area were raped in their apartments. Another woman disappeared from her apartment without a trace. Investigators from the Monroe County Sheriff's Office, Greece Police Department and Gates Police Department teamed up to investigate and arrest the person or persons responsible.

Our first case was a burglary-rape that occurred in the town of Henrietta. My partner, Tom Vasile, and I responded to the early morning call out. A single mother of two was raped in her apartment by a stranger upon her return home from an evening out with her co-workers and friends. Her children were not home at the time. From law enforcement's point of view, these are some of the most vicious crimes committed against a person and some of the most difficult to solve. A large percentage of rapes are committed by someone known by or at least familiar to the victim. These are easier cases to resolve by an arrest, as the positive identification of the perpetrator is not an issue. When the victim does not know her attacker, it is more challenging for law enforcement to prove. Until the perpetrator can be identified and apprehended, the victim bears an added trauma: she is forced to live with the knowledge that her assailant is still lurking about and could attack her again at any time.

Most convicts have family members of their own that they care about in the outside world. They worry about the safety of their mothers, sisters, daughters or wives, just as we do. They recognize that the tree jumper could very well attack one of their loved ones, for jumpers randomly choose victims that they do not know. Next to child molesters, rapists are the most hated criminals in a prison population, often suffering some form of retribution at the hands of other convicts.

The victim's apartment was located in a large complex on the south side of Monroe County, which is widely known for its large population of retail stores, restaurants and one of the area's major shopping malls. This area borders the New York State Thruway, making it easily accessible to interstate-traveling, transient types. The victim had already been transported to the hospital by the time Tom Vasile and I arrived on scene. The patrol deputies and command officers at the crime scene advised us of the circumstances of the attack, which apparently lasted most of the night and early morning. It appeared that the perpetrator was already in the apartment, awaiting the victim's return. Hearing this fact made my mind drift to how afraid my wife is to enter our darkened home alone at night. That nightmarish thought turned into a horrible reality for this single working mother.

The apartment was very clean and well kept. The first responding deputy informed us that, according to the victim, when the perpetrator first attacked and blindfolded her, he wore a hockey goalie mask similar to the one worn by the Jason character in the *Friday the 13th* horror movies. We saw a pull cord from the window blinds in the living room lying on the floor of the victim's bedroom. It had been used to tie her hands to the headboard of her bed. Certain places in the apartment had been wiped clean by the perpetrator, and he had forced the victim to shower and wash her bedsheets after the attack. These chilling facts led us to conclude that the rapist had already done hard time in prison for sexual assault and most likely had been convicted by trace evidence. It was obvious to Tom and me that we were after a genuine tree jumper who had perfected his sick game.

A canvass of the apartment building and surrounding buildings turned up nothing conclusive, just a report of a suspicious vehicle seen in the area a few days earlier. The description did not include a license plate number. Our preliminary investigation produced nothing more than a severely traumatized victim who was barely able to talk about the attack and the realization that we had no evidence to work with and no leads to follow.

On Memorial Day weekend, Tom and I were called in from home early in the morning to the scene of another attack at an apartment complex in the town of Penfield. This time there were two victims, a single mother and her teenage daughter. The mother was sitting up in bed watching the late news when her daughter arrived home after going out to dinner with her school friends. The daughter was excited about the upcoming school prom; they sat on her bed together and talked about those preparations that moms and daughters love to discuss. They shared an intimate moment that was meant to be a joyful memory in both of their lives for years to come. This precious memory was stolen by an evil criminal.

The daughter retired to her room for the night across the hall from her mother's bedroom, which was on the second floor of the two-story, townhouse-style apartment. The mother recalled sitting up in bed reading a book while *The Tonight Show* with Johnny Carson played on the television when she noticed a large, masked figure standing in her bedroom doorway. Without saying a word, the intruder jumped onto her and began attacking her. I will spare you the gruesome details and simply share that this animal tied up the mother and her daughter in their respective bedrooms and sexually assaulted both of them. Each victim could hear the other being assaulted throughout this horrific night. Every time I think about this case it pierces my heart. I think of how my own daughters and wife bask in the safety and sanctity of our home, enjoying many special mother-daughter

Village of Penfield: one of the suburban towns that Ed Laraby drove through, seeking his next victim. *Courtesy of Gene Renner.*

moments. The thought of this mother and daughter being violently attacked in what is supposed to be their personal haven and robbed of those cherished moments fills me with anger and hatred.

Once again, the perp did not leave us any clues to work with. A neighborhood canvass was fruitless, and there was no physical evidence. We were left with nothing but our own seething anger and a burning desire to keep seeking answers. Since we had nothing tangible to further our investigations, Tom and I reached out to the other police agencies in the area. We soon learned that the Gates Police Department was investigating a rape that appeared to be similar in modus operandi, otherwise known as MO. The victim lived alone in an apartment complex and was attacked by an unknown intruder who spent most of the night sexually assaulting her. The perpetrator did not leave behind any workable evidence. The assailants in the Henrietta, Penfield and Gates attacks were all described as Caucasians with large builds.

We also learned that the Greece Police Department was investigating the report of a missing young woman who lived alone in an apartment complex in their town. She was a young music teacher with a promising career and bright future ahead of her. Her vehicle was later found at the Greater Rochester International Airport. The investigation was a high-profile item in the media, receiving headline coverage for a sustained period of time. Much to their credit, the police in Greece were not showing their hand, which left the case open to much public speculation.

During their missing person investigation, the detectives from Greece had discovered that a man named Ed Laraby was employed at the apartment complex where the missing woman lived. Mr. Laraby, a Caucasian with red hair and a large build, was currently on parole for robbery. Back in 1983, he attacked a mother and her teenage daughter while they were walking on the canal path, a popular hiking and biking trail that runs along the historic and picturesque Erie Canal. During the attack, Laraby wore one of those horrific-looking rubber Halloween masks, jumped out of the bushes, grabbed the woman's daughter and held a knife to her throat. Then he tied their hands together and robbed them. Further background investigation revealed that Laraby had been sent to prison after raping a fifteen-year-old girl and a seventeen-year-old girl in separate incidents in 1973. While wearing a ski mask, he kidnapped the fifteen-year-old at knife point, bound and gagged her and then cut her clothes off with the knife. Laraby forced the seventeen-year-old into his vehicle as she was walking in a populated commercial area and then drove her to a secluded area and raped her. Both crimes occurred in two of the more affluent eastside communities of Monroe County.

Photo of the historic Erie Canal, where Ed Laraby attacked some of his first victims as they walked along the canal path. *Courtesy of Gene Renner.*

In 1980, Laraby's conviction was reversed on a legal technicality, and he was released from prison. Shortly after his release, Laraby abducted another teenage girl at knife point, tied her up and then forced her to commit oral sex on him. Incredulously, the judge released him after his arraignment. Laraby then attempted to escape to Canada, but he was arrested at the border. He later pleaded guilty to the attack and was sentenced to two to seven years of incarceration. Shortly after his reincarceration, he was released yet again on a legal technicality that had nothing to do with his innocence or guilt. This left him free to continue to offend until he was arrested for the aforementioned attacks on the canal path in 1983.

Based upon his criminal history, MO and employment connection to the apartment complex of the missing woman, Ed Laraby was turning out to be a viable suspect. Additional facts made him look even better: we had a perpetrator who was making his victims clean up after the sexual assaults, indicative of a criminal who had been educated about the legal importance of physical evidence; and while the victims were unable to positively identify their masked assailant, they described him as a large white male. Laraby was big, and he liked to use masks during his attacks.

Other graphic facts made him a likely suspect for these crimes. The despicable things that the perp did to the victims during these assaults were similar in the three cases and appeared to have been learned from a prison environment. Anyone who has served hard time in prison knows all too well that convicts are violently raped and sodomized by other convicts. There are certain things that occur during those sexual assaults that are specific to that particular environment. Consequently, many convicts adopt those behaviors and continue them upon their release back into society. The detective who frequently conducts investigations of reported sexual assaults can recognize these very distinctive signatures while debriefing a victim about the nature of the assault and the assailant. Based on what we had learned about Ed Laraby, he fit the bill in all aspects of these cases.

We had to come up with a plan on how we were going to investigate Mr. Laraby as a potential suspect and not miss the opportunity to arrest him if it should arise. That was much easier said than done. Mr. Laraby, as we knew from his past, did not talk to the police. So picking him up for an interview was not a viable option. He would most likely invoke his right to a lawyer and remain silent, and he would stop the attacks since he would know that we were on to him. And since none of the police agencies had any physical evidence to compare with a potential suspect, there was no way to corroborate our theory yet.

We were left with two options: set up surveillance on as many apartment complexes as possible in the area of Monroe County, which wasn't feasible based on the huge amount of manpower and resources that would be needed, or conduct a physical surveillance on Mr. Laraby. Following him around until he attacked his next victim was not an easy option either. Doing that without the suspect finding out is nearly impossible if you don't have a small army to do it with, and that wasn't going to happen. Nevertheless, with what we knew, we couldn't just sit around and do nothing. So each of the police departments designated a few investigators, and together we kept Mr. Laraby under surveillance during the evening hours.

Our team of seven investigators monitored the suspect seven days a week, from 8:00 p.m. until he went home for the night. He worked the B shift (3:00 p.m. to 11:00 p.m.) at a local machine shop on the west side of the city. We quickly learned that he liked to frequent several bars in the area, drinking for a few hours, in violation of his parole, and then he would go out hunting for his next potential victim. On the nights that he didn't work, Mr. Laraby stayed close to home.

Laraby lived in a modest residential neighborhood in the town of Greece, which is in the northwest area of Monroe County. A large Marriott Hotel housed a popular nightclub near his residence. Across the street from the club was a supermarket parking lot that proved to be a convenient location for many of the nightclub's patrons to hook up after the bar closed. Because the surveillance team staged in that parking lot when Laraby was at home, we obtained an uncensored insight into human behavior in the underworld of those looking for love in all of the wrong places. We wondered how they would feel if they knew that seven undercover cops were observing their every move.

During that particular summer, the Rochester area was blitzed with frequent and severe lightning storms, most of which occurred during the evening. The violent weather exacerbated my family's stress over my nighttime absences. My wife and young children were terrified and hardly slept a wink that summer. It didn't help that our house was struck by lightning twice during that time. Once, a large flame shot out of the wall light switch in our front foyer. The intense heat melted it, causing the house to reek of melted plastic and burning electrical wires. We even had to call the fire department to make sure that a fire wasn't smoldering in our walls.

For the first three weeks of surveillance, Laraby stuck to the same pattern. Because of all the media attention on the apartment complex rapes and added police patrols, he steered clear of those locations. Instead, he started driving around residential neighborhoods, peering into windows of single-family dwellings. It was very stressful to watch such a criminal engage in this type of behavior, knowing what he was capable of doing to another human being. If we lost him or miscalculated his movements, he might have raped or even murdered a woman right under our noses. This was something that none of us wanted to have on our consciences.

By his movements and driving patterns, it appeared that Ed was getting restless and wanted some action. This, I believe, led him to the Lyell Avenue area, which is one of several locations in the city where one can meet a prostitute who will take a ride with them. Sometime around 3:00 a.m., near the end of our shift, Ed ended up pulling over and picking up a white female prostitute. He drove her to an industrial area on the west side of the city between Gates and Greece. We lost him and were unable to locate his truck for fifteen minutes. We were extremely dismayed, for that window of opportunity provided a criminal like Laraby enough time to choke someone and hastily dump their body. The fact that the woman was a prostitute did not make her life any less important. Her life hung in the balance, and we had to find him.

As I drove down one of the streets in the area with all of the windows down, I heard a woman screaming. The road was very dark because there wasn't much traffic nor were there many street lights. I stopped the car to listen. Then, out of the darkness, a young woman ran up to my car from behind one of the buildings, begging me to help her, screaming "He's trying to kill me!" Before I had time to respond, she jumped into the front passenger seat and yelled, "Get going! He's going to kill us!"

At this moment I observed a large figure running along the road in the dark up ahead of us. I was unable to grab my portable radio to call for backup because the terrified woman had sat on it when she jumped into the car. Not wanting to lose sight of Ed running away, I gave chase by driving the car up next to him as he was running. I then hit the brakes hard just ahead of him and jumped out to meet him.

Since I was alone and it was dark, I drew my 9 mm pistol on him, ordering him to stop. Ed stopped, but he appeared to be intoxicated. He started getting belligerent with me, making movements with his hands toward his waistband like he was trying to grab something. Since he was wearing an unbuttoned flannel shirt over a T-shirt, I couldn't see if anything was there. He turned halfway around like he was going to take off and then I noticed a bulge in the small of his back under the flannel shirt. This increased my sense of alarm. I ordered him to turn around, and I felt the instinctive movement of my finger starting to gently pull the hammer of my pistol back as Ed turned and faced me.

Ed then made a half-hearted attempt to get around the front of my car. Not wanting him to escape, but not having the legal authority to shoot him if he fled, I lunged and shoved him over the hood of my car. Being a big guy, Ed was hard to control once I had him on the hood. I had limited use of my strong hand, which was still holding my service weapon. Wrestling someone with a gun in one hand creates a grave risk for the policeman. A handgun is not loyal to its owner like a police dog: it will turn on you if it gets into the perpetrator's hands. Laraby was a heavy, strong guy with nothing to lose. Praise the Lord, a partner and friend, Glen Grana, arrived on the scene just as I was taking Ed down over the hood. Glen assisted me with gaining control and handcuffing him.

The victim had been screaming hysterically as she sat in the car while I was trying to get control of Ed, not realizing that we were the police until the event was over. After she finally calmed down, I informed her that we needed to talk to her. The prostitute, who identified herself as "Kim," was reluctant to cooperate, but she did share that Ed had driven her behind one of the buildings. After he parked the truck, they stepped out and sat on a picnic table to have sex. When Ed started to act abusive, Kim called the deal off and gave Ed his twelve dollars back. When she attempted to leave, Ed wrapped his big arm around her tiny neck and began choking her. Kim said that her feet were dangling in the air as she struggled to break loose. By the look of Ed's face and neck, Kim must have fought like a frenzied polecat during the attack. Ed then threw her violently to the ground. At this point she began pleading with him, and he stopped the attack for a moment. That's when Kim made the move that saved her life: she got up and ran, screaming for help.

Typical of these incidents, the prostitute did not want to pursue criminal charges against her attacker. She demanded that we either release her or arrest her. We contacted Chuck Siragusa, who was the first assistant to the Monroe County district attorney at the time (he now serves as a federal judge in the U.S. District Court of Western New York). Unfortunately, he told us what we already knew—without the cooperation of the young prostitute, we had no case against Mr. Laraby. So we let her go. Now the question was, what should we do with Ed? And what type of explanation were we going to offer him as to why undercover police officers were there to rescue the young prostitute? We transported him to my office to afford me more time to think.

With a smirk on his lips and an overly friendly tone, Ed admitted meeting the prostitute for sex. He acknowledged that he had paid her but claimed that she had tried to steal money from him while they were taking their pants off. Mr. Laraby's story wasn't far-fetched, for prostitutes are known to steal from their solicitors (also known as johns). I allowed him to believe that his slick buddy-buddy approach was softening me up. He then politely invoked his right to an attorney and refused to speak with us about the matter any further.

I told Mr. Laraby that we were operating a hooker detail along Lyell Avenue. I also explained that while he had gotten caught in our web, since we were unable to catch them in the act, we were going to cut him some slack and let him go. He asked me if I was going to call his parole officer. I told him that I wouldn't; however, he'd owe me a favor sometime in the future. I then supplied him with the information that he needed to retrieve his truck from the auto impound. Aside from the inconvenience and a stiff towing and storage fee, Mr. Laraby got away with attempted murder. Two members of the team, Glen Grana and Bob Trowbridge, drove Ed home, and we called it a wrap for the night, which had already turned into morning.

Ed laid low for the next several days after he paid to get his truck out of the auto pound. We figured that he didn't have any money to go out drinking after work. So it made for any easy week, just hanging out and watching the rain pound on our windshields, listening to Dr. Ruth talk to sexually troubled people on late-night radio. We ate a lot of ice cream and other forbidden foods like pizza, burgers, hot dogs and Buffalo-style chicken wings. What a life. While the rest of the world was sleeping, here we were: sitting in our undercover vehicles in a deserted parking lot in the middle of the night, watching ground-shaking thunderstorms blow in and out, eating junk food and listening to a seventy-year-old woman talk about sex and masturbation on the radio to stay awake. Only in police work.

Within a week or so, Ed was on the move again. He started leaving work at 11:00 p.m. and trolling the city nightclub district in search of potential victims. Once again, we stalked the predator as he stalked his prey. Ed stayed away from the prostitutes, just as I had directed him. This time his travel appeared to be focused on the east side of the city and county.

About six weeks into our surveillance detail, Ed made his move. We were in the downtown nightclub district, near a bar called Heaven, which was a popular hangout for college students and younger adults. On weekend nights, the club crowd usually spilled over into the small side street and sidewalk. Ed would continually drive around a few blocks, lurking and looking, slowly moving in and out of traffic. He liked to park his truck and just watch his potential prey parade by, totally unaware of the danger that

*Opposite, above and below*: These are photos of the downtown Rochester area where Ed Laraby was under surveillance while he hunted for his next rape victim. *Courtesy of Gene Renner.*

was just a few feet away. Ed's actions resembled those of a great white shark swimming among other species when he drove around this area. If some of these seductively dressed young women had only known how close they were to a rapist and suspected murderer during those summer nights. We were afraid that Ed would just open his truck door and yank one of these unsuspecting young women into his truck and force her down onto the floor. This was a real concern because Ed's truck wasn't always in our sight. Being downtown, it was difficult to stay close to him without crossing his line of vision. While he didn't appear too concerned about whether he was being followed, Ed would get nervous if he observed the same vehicles and drivers showing up around him. It was a delicate balance to maintain—to stay loose enough to allow our target enough room to make his move but close enough to not lose him without blowing our cover. I could only hope and pray that we would be right there when he pounced. Knowing that a kidnapping and violent assault could literally occur right under our noses was a serious concern for all of us. First, I give credit to God for our success in preventing such a tragedy from occurring. Secondly, I give credit to the members of the surveillance team for their skill and professionalism under extreme pressure and not blowing our cover and the entire operation.

Ed picked out a potential victim: a petite young woman with long, curly blonde hair, wearing skintight spandex pants and stiletto heels. She was walking away from the nightclub during the late evening hours. He continued to slowly drive around each block, circling and stalking her, as she continued eastbound on East Avenue. East Avenue is lined with ornate street lamps and beautiful old mansions with large manicured yards. It was once home to George Eastman, the founder of Eastman Kodak, and it continues to serve as home for many of the wealthy in our area. Incredibly, this petite young woman walked out of the downtown district by herself on the sidewalk that follows along historical East Avenue.

Laraby eventually parked his truck on one of the side streets that connects East Avenue with Park Avenue and started following his prey on foot. We watched him slowly gain ground on the unsuspecting woman as she continued walking eastbound. Once she was walking through a long stretch of darkness provided by some heavy foliage, Ed made his move. He ran up from behind her and wrapped his arm around her neck. The force of his attack lifted the victim's feet right off the ground, and he pulled her into some shrubs adjacent to the sidewalk. At that point they were out of our sight. There were some large trees on the other side of the shrubs that provided plenty of concealment for the ongoing attack.

East Avenue area of Rochester: area where Ed Laraby was under surveillance as he stalked and attacked a woman who turned out to be a petite man dressed in drag. *Courtesy of Gene Renner.*

The stress we were experiencing at this moment was like nothing I had ever experienced. Here we had a vicious predator beginning to devour a victim right under our noses, and we had to stand by just long enough to allow him the time to start tearing her clothes off to show his intent to sexually assault her. This victim was not just a decoy we were using to catch this monster—she was someone's child and loved one. As we prepared to close in and stop the attack, I started the "one–one thousand count" to ten and was about halfway through it when Laraby bolted from the bushes, ran back to his truck and drove off. I directed the team not to follow him. We could grab him anytime. Instead, we ran to assist the victim who had not reappeared from the shrubs. Once again, I was worried that something went terribly wrong and Laraby had seriously injured or killed her. It only takes a second to snap someone's neck or plunge a knife into their chest cavity.

By the time we reached the victim, she was back on her feet and attempting to make her way out of the foliage. Thank God, she didn't appear to be seriously injured, just shaken up. We immediately determined why Ed aborted his attack and ran like a bolt of lightning. This little blonde bombshell in the tight spandex pants and high heels had five o'clock shadow growing on her face and an Adam's apple protruding from her throat. She was, in fact, a he. We could do nothing but laugh, wondering what went through Laraby's mind when he felt the man's beard stubble beneath his hand as he was forcefully pressing it over his mouth. I would have loved to see the expression on Ed's face at that moment.

Once again, God was on our side. Had we closed in on Laraby too quickly, we would have exposed our surveillance of him and blown the whole case. It was literally a matter of another two seconds. Once we made sure that our cross-dressing, alternative-lifestyle citizen was safely transported home, the team confirmed that Laraby drove directly to his residence after his failed attempt. I figured that if there were ever a time that Laraby would wonder if he should pack it in and go straight, this would have been it.

True to form, Ed laid low for another week or so before he started getting active again. We endured another several days of sitting around a deserted parking lot watching unsuspecting bar patrons from the Marriott Hotel hooking up in their cars to fornicate the night away in front of a half-dozen undercover cops. Instead of listening to Dr. Ruth on the radio, I managed to catch up on my recreational reading.

Sometime around the seventh week of our surveillance detail, Ed got his mojo back and was getting antsy. Once again, he started going out drinking and cruising after work. It was obvious that despite his two failed attempts that included a stern warning from the police to stay out of trouble, Ed couldn't control his desire to hunt and rape women. It was as if he were possessed by some evil demon that could only be satisfied by the violent act of rape.

Laraby would periodically park in a residential neighborhood and exit his truck. After hanging out around the truck for a few minutes, probably to see if he was being followed, he would walk around and peer into house windows. We figured that he was trying to find a female that was home alone. It was pretty wild to watch this man hide in the bushes next to a house, staring into the window. Ed liked to choose houses that were surrounded with plenty of bushes and trees, for they served as great cover for him. For whatever reason, Laraby never attempted to enter one of those dwellings while he was under our surveillance. I am thankful for that. Had we been forced to go into a residence after him, it would have presented a very dangerous situation. He could have easily taken the victim hostage in a dark house that was unfamiliar to us. Also, if Laraby had entered someone's home while we were conducting a physical surveillance on him, it would have been a public relations disaster for the Monroe County Sheriff. How could we justify allowing Laraby to commit the crime of burglary in order to build

Spawn of Satan

a criminal case, instead of protecting the person that was inside the home? To prevent this PR nightmare, we would have had to grab Laraby just as he was in the process of breaking in. This would have allowed us to charge him with attempted burglary of a residence, which is considered a felony in New York State. Anything short of that would be a misdemeanor and would not have accomplished our goal of locking this guy up for a long period of time.

So the pressure was on us to not prematurely close in on him and blow the case. We had to allow him the opportunity to start breaking in but not allow him to gain entry into the home and take a potential hostage. The window of opportunity would only be open for a second or two to decide whether we should close in. It didn't help matters that we had to allow Laraby enough lead time so that he didn't observe us following him. The darkness, heavy rain and the dark shadows of shrubs and trees made an already difficult surveillance task nearly impossible. The members of our team were extremely good at keeping their cool. If there was ever a time that we could have blown this case, it was during these very tense moments. Thanks to the competence and professionalism of my peers and the grace of God, that did not happen.

After about nine nerve-wracking and wearisome weeks, our patience finally paid off. In the early morning of August 14, 1992, Ed Laraby attacked again, and we were there to stop him. As he did many times in the past, Laraby was driving around and looking for potential prey after he got out of work the previous evening. The surveillance team lost Laraby at 11:35 p.m. in the area of Main and Broad Streets downtown. It wasn't until around 1:30 a.m. that we located his truck parked outside a saloon in East Rochester, which is about ten miles east of the city. These two hours out of our sight provided plenty of time to rape a victim and then go to a bar to revel in success and tie one on.

Laraby exited the bar at about 2:25 a.m. and got into his truck. He then drove to the Wegman's Supermarket on Fairport Road and went into the store. Ten minutes later, Laraby went back to his truck and drove westbound on Monroe Avenue until he pulled into the parking lot of a fast-food restaurant. Laraby remained in his truck and turned the lights off. After sitting there for a moment, he continued driving westbound on Monroe Avenue. It was obvious to us that Ed was trying to figure out if he was being followed. His furtive behavior led us to believe that he was up to something.

Laraby continued westbound on Monroe Avenue well into the city and then turned left onto Field Street, which is just east of the Interstate 490 junction with Monroe Avenue. In close proximity of that intersection was Grana's Restaurant,

Monroe Avenue and Shepard Street: the location where Ed Laraby stalked and attacked his last victim. He was arrested during that attack. *Courtesy of Gene Renner.*

which was owned by one of the surveillance team members' uncles. I observed Laraby hawking two teenage females walking eastbound along Monroe Avenue in front of the restaurant, so I alerted the team that Laraby might be going around the block to do another drive-by. As suspected, Laraby turned back onto Monroe Avenue and drove by the two girls again as they continued walking eastbound on the sidewalk. Laraby then turned down a side street that was east of the females' location. He parked and continued the hunt on foot.

At first, Laraby walked eastbound on the sidewalk along Monroe Avenue, maintaining a position in front of the girls. It appeared that they didn't even notice that he was walking ahead of them. We figured that Laraby was looking for a place to hide himself, hoping that the girls would separate somewhere along the way. Moments later, Laraby did an about-face and began walking in a westbound direction directly toward the girls, who still appeared unaware of him. When Laraby met up with the girls on the sidewalk, he continued walking right past them. Again, neither girl appeared to pay any attention as they passed. Laraby acted like a shark, greedily circling closer to its victim in anticipation of a fatal strike.

Just as we have seen numerous times on television shows that document the life and habits of various predators in the wild kingdom, Laraby did a second about-face and picked up his pace. He then broke into a short sprint toward his two unsuspecting victims and violently grabbed one from behind. Laraby wrapped one of his big arms around her neck and placed her in a chokehold. With his other hand he reached between the young woman's legs and grabbed her pubic area from behind. The force of the attack lifted the young woman's feet clear off the ground. Laraby then attempted to drag her backward, but the young woman fought back and was able to break free as Laraby stumbled. He let go and began running back to his truck—but it was too late. We closed in on Big Ed this time and took him down on the front lawn of a house on Monroe Avenue. He put up a little bit of a fight, but he was no match for the likes of Investigators Bob Trowbridge, who reached him first, and Al Krause, affectionately known as "The Goon."

Because Laraby was combative even after he was handcuffed, we called for the city paddy wagon after the show up was completed. (That is where the victim is given a chance to look at the suspect and tell the police whether that was the person who attacked her.) It wasn't really necessary since we had at least six cops who witnessed the attack, but we did it anyway. It couldn't hurt our case. During the show up, Laraby thrashed back and forth as Bob Trowbridge and I attempted to hold him still. Laraby kept saying, "just shoot me—just shoot me," repeatedly. Big Ed knew that he was going down. He

had been caught fair and square in the middle of attacking another woman and attempting to kidnap and sexually assault her.

Upon its arrival, Laraby was placed inside the police wagon, where he was alone. He then proceeded to smash his face into a bloody pulp against the diamond-plated steel floor, yelling, "Police brutality!" We didn't try to restrain him. In fact, we laughed at Laraby and photographed him during his tantrum to prove that we did not serve him any

Mug shot of Ed Laraby. *Courtesy of the Monroe County Sheriff's Office.*

CHRONICLES OF A ROCHESTER MAJOR CRIMES DETECTIVE

curbside justice. The team members handled themselves like professionals and avoided any heavy-handed tactics with Laraby in spite of his antics.

Eventually, Laraby ran out of gas and settled down. By the look of his face, he must have felt like someone hit him with a sledgehammer. We offered to take him to a hospital for treatment of his self-inflicted facial lacerations, but he refused, so we took him directly to jail. It was obvious that Laraby wanted his arrest mug shot to look as bad as it could so that he could accuse us of giving him a good, old-fashioned police beating, but our photographs proved otherwise.

After we took detailed statements from our victim and her friend, we drove them home. I think it was about 7:00 a.m. when we finally called it a night. Because of how forcefully he grabbed the victim, we were able to charge Laraby with sexual abuse in the first degree, which is a violent sex offense. Had Ed not grabbed her by the pubic area while he was choking and dragging her away, we would not have been able to charge him with a felony.

Monroe County assistant district attorney Ken Hyland was assigned to prosecute this case. Laraby retained Mike Schiano as his defense attorney. As we were preparing for trial, Mr. Schiano advised Ken that Laraby wanted to work out a deal. Laraby offered to provide information regarding the whereabouts of the missing music teacher if the district attorney's office was willing to give him a lighter sentence. Laraby did not intend to confess to the kidnapping or murder of the young woman but rather preface his information as secondhand. The Monroe County District Attorney's Office rejected Laraby's offer for the obvious reason that he was the leading suspect in that investigation. It was difficult to deny the young woman's family the ability to locate their daughter, but there was no way that we could give Ed Laraby a free pass for what we believed to be her murder.

Fortunately, even without his "generous offer," the woman's body was located a few years later. It was discovered in a creek bed west of Rochester. That was consistent with the thoughts of a confidential informant close to Laraby and his family, who said that Ed liked to fish and had a small fishing boat. They had always thought that the young teacher's remains were buried somewhere near a body of water or at the bottom of a lake.

While Laraby was awaiting trial, we were alerted by the Monroe County Jail Bureau Command Staff that Laraby was planning to escape. He made the mistake of sharing his plan with another inmate who happened to be a trustee (someone who receives extra privileges for assisting the jail staff with duties in their cell block). The trustee told a deputy that Laraby planned to assault and overpower a female deputy and take her keys. Laraby expected to gain entry to one of the offices that has a window to the outside and then lower himself to the ground with some bedding tied together. This elevated his inmate status to high risk. As a result, he was placed in a "box" and kept under twenty-four-hour surveillance. He was accompanied by extra jail guards during his court appearances and wore shackles around his ankles.

When Laraby's trial finally started months later, the people of New York were very limited as to what they could present as evidence. Assistant District Attorney Ken Hyland was not allowed to demonstrate that the police had developed Ed Laraby as a suspect in connection to the apartment break-in rapes earlier that year nor could he share with the jury that the police spent nine weeks following Laraby, witnessing him stalk numerous potential victims and attack two other people. He also was not allowed to share that Laraby had previously been sent to prison after being convicted of raping and sodomizing other women. In other words, the case was presented as though we were a bunch of cops who, by chance, happened to be at the right place at the right time and observed this animal violently attack a young woman as she walked down the street with her friend. The court ruled that the aforementioned information would be prejudicial to the defendant and prevent him from receiving a fair trial.

New York State Supreme Court justice Eugene Bergin presided over the trial. Justice Bergin was a solid judge and kept the trial on track. I testified at the trial along with some of the other members of the surveillance and arrest team. The case was presented to the twelve jurors and two alternate jurors without a hitch, and they convicted Laraby for sexual abuse in the first degree. Before the jury was excused, Justice Bergin met with them along with the prosecutor to answer any questions or concerns they had.

According to Ken Hyland, Justice Bergin took the opportunity to praise the jury for their decision to convict Laraby on what little evidence that was allowed to be presented. Justice Bergin advised the jury about Laraby's violent past and how the police had developed him as a suspect and had been following him for the entire summer. Justice Bergin closed his comments by telling the jury that they did Monroe County and New York State a great service by convicting him of this crime. Needless to say, Justice Bergin sentenced Ed Laraby as a triple-predicate violent felon (aka "three-time loser") and ordered him to serve twenty-five years in the custody of the New York State Department of Corrections.

Our command officers, Chief Anthony Ciaccia and Captain Cornelius Flood, contributed greatly to the success of this case by their patience and willingness to maintain faith in their detectives throughout the investigation and surveillance operation. Without it, this case would not have ended with a successful disposition. This type of aggressive police work is not for the weak of heart, and anything short of strong leadership makes it very difficult for any criminal investigator to be effective, no matter how good they are. The leaders who empower those who serve beneath them will always enjoy more success.

Several years later, I was contacted by a New York State Police investigator stationed in Auburn. He advised me that Ed Laraby had suffered chest pains while in the Auburn State Prison. While he was being evaluated at the hospital, Laraby attacked the armed prison guard that was accompanying him. During the protracted physical struggle, Laraby wrapped a cord connected to his hospital bed around the neck of the much smaller prison guard and began to choke him out while reaching for his handgun. The prison guard was able to pull his service weapon and break free from his would-be killer's chokehold and thwart his attempted escape until the police arrived. State Police investigator David Stebbins, who looked into the incident, advised that Laraby was arrested and subsequently tried and convicted of attempted murder in the first degree and attempted escape. He was sentenced to an additional twenty-five years to life, to be served consecutively when his first life sentence runs out.

ADA Ken Hyland said that he was relieved to know that Laraby was not going to be eligible for parole until he was old enough to be back in diapers. Mr. Hyland has put many dangerous people in prison over the past two decades. While he is rarely intimidated by these thugs, he believes that Laraby is the only criminal that he ever prosecuted who would seek revenge after his release against those responsible for putting him in prison.

Until I crossed paths with Ed Laraby, I had never seen evil up close and personal. And as of this writing, I have yet to encounter anyone as dangerous as this man. I have investigated and arrested numerous sick, degenerate types who have committed unthinkable crimes against others, but I have never been amid such evil as when I was in the presence of Ed Laraby. This man is a predator of the female gender and an enemy of the human race.

*Case 4*
# Murder in Pittsford

*Speak up for those who cannot speak for themselves;*
*ensure justice for those being crushed.*
—*Proverbs 31:8*

L ieutenant Charles Schirtz was on the other end of the call when I responded to the page from my home at nine o'clock that night. His voice was both serious and somber. Lieutenant Schirtz had just transferred from the patrol division, where he spent the majority of his career since we had graduated from the police academy together over two decades earlier, to take the administrative lieutenant day slot in the Criminal Investigative Division.

Nobody looked better in a navy blue police uniform than Lieutenant Schirtz. He could have easily been cast as a member of Hitler's chosen race for a Hollywood World War II movie. He is an imposing figure who keeps his light hair high and tight and peers at you with intense blue eyes. His laugh is both loud and infectious. Even though our careers had taken two distinctively different paths since working the midnight patrol shift together as rookie deputies in the "Old Zone B," I still considered him a trusted friend and was glad he chose to put on a suit for a while.

Lieutenant Schirtz, who I affectionately called "Chuck" or "Charlie," advised that an eighty-six-year-old woman was found strangled and stabbed to death in her apartment in the upscale town of Pittsford. Murders were not supposed to happen in the wealthiest town of Monroe County. That was one of the main reasons people paid the incredibly high property taxes to reside there. Chuck said the perpetrator was not in custody nor was a specific person suspected. This murder was not only brutal and senseless, it was a real "who dun it?"

Chuck said the patrol commander thought the murder may have been the result of a "follow-home robbery" where the perpetrator targets elderly folks from a shopping center or doctor's office and follows them home to rob them as they enter their residence. The crimes are committed in the privacy of the victims' own homes, usually with no witnesses.

Like young children, elderly people usually prove to be ill-equipped witnesses due to their inability to observe and remember. These circumstances make them a favorite target of the predatory violent criminals in our modern society. Similar to predators in the animal kingdom, human predators stalk and pursue the weak and frailest of their kind to devour and consume, for they offer little if any resistance.

Having said that, the murder of an elderly person can challenge the emotional strength of the most callous Major Crimes–homicide detectives. It is comparable to the killing of a child. Both age groups are the most vulnerable in our communities. They are the helpless and defenseless ones who rely on others to keep them safe. To harm one of them is one of the lowest acts a human can do.

Resolved to the fact that I was looking at another sleepless night, I got dressed, left a note for my family, who was out for the evening, and drove out of the driveway in my unmarked Ford Crown Victoria. I pulled into a large gas station along the way to grab a cup of hot black coffee to get my slumbering brain jump-started for the task at hand. The combination of cool air of the fall evening and the caffeine enabled me to catch my second wind by the time I arrived on the scene.

The apartment building that housed the victim was located on the east end of the large apartment complex. The road that led up to the contemporary brick structure was choked off by a parade of marked and unmarked sheriffs' cars parked bumper to bumper, requiring me to park my vehicle nearly half a football field away from the building's front entrance. I took in the whole scene as I walked up to the huddle of command personnel forming on the sidewalk that led up to the front exterior steps of the building. Lieutenant Schirtz arrived on scene around the same time I did.

Investigator Dave Vaughn arrived minutes after me, making us the first two Major Crimes detectives on scene. Lieutenant Schirtz promptly assigned us to be the lead detectives on the case. What this meant was everything would work through Investigator Vaughn and me from that point on.

We had been advised that the victim was discovered by her neighbor after the woman's son had called her to check on his mother, who uncharacteristically had not responded to his telephone calls that evening. The neighbor, a middle-aged woman, used the extra key that had been given to her by the victim's son months earlier to enter the apartment and found the victim where she lay. The neighbor reportedly called 911 and advised the victim's son of what she had discovered.

After the briefing, Dave and I nonchalantly drifted from the crowd of decision makers and moved toward the entrance. A crime scene technician confirmed that the area had been photographed as he exited the building and walked past us. I won't enter a homicide scene until it has been frozen in time with photographs.

"You ready to take a look inside before this gets all fucked up?" Dave asked in his usual sarcastic tone.

"Lead the way," I said, as we made our way up the front steps.

Sleek as a racing greyhound K-9, Investigator Dave Vaughn stands approximately six feet, four inches tall with a basketball player's physique. He has sandy brown hair and a handsome face of sharp features that easily expresses his emotional state at any given moment. Many of those expressions are accentuated by a sarcastic comment of disgust that usually results from Dave being agitated by a victim who is being less than honest or directives passed down by police management. The other thing about "Big Dave" is that he is the best dresser in the unit.

Dave and I checked in with the uniformed deputy posted at the apartment door keeping a written log of who was entering and exiting the victim's apartment. I placed my hands in my coat pockets as I stepped inside. I examined the door's latch and observed no evidence of a forced entry. The deputy confirmed that this was the only entrance to the apartment. There was no fire escape since the dwelling was considered to be on the first floor.

By the layout of the scene, it appeared our victim, *Rose Sweet, was attacked as she answered the door. She was lying faceup on the plush white carpet in the short entrance hallway that opened up to the combination living and dining room area of the apartment. Her slippers were near to the door, which indicated she was attacked in such a forceful and violent manner that as she opened the door it knocked her out of her slippers.

It appeared the woman had been strangled to death and then stabbed multiple times about her chest and throat. There was a minimal loss of blood since her heart had already stopped from the strangulation. The first responding deputy said the paramedics that responded to the scene had cut

*Above and below*: Village of Pittsford and Pittsford Estates. *Courtesy of Gene Renner.*

the victim's white, blood-soaked blouse up the middle when they attempted to revive her.

The victim's face was red and swollen, and both of her hands were closed in a clutch position, resting against her chest. A clump of her white hair was located on the floor between her head and an ironing board stand that flanked her body's left side. The victim's eyes and mouth were open. By the expression on her face, she suffered a terrifying death.

An unplugged electric iron was lying on the floor beneath it. By the imprint observed on the surface of the ironing board, it appeared the iron had been resting on top of it and was knocked off during the attack. There was a small plant in a ceramic pot that was knocked over on its side, lying on the floor next to the victim's right side. I observed what appeared to be a small smudge located on the corner of the wall just above the knocked over plant.

Items observed on the dining table led us to believe the victim was eating her dinner just prior to the attack. I observed light-red smudges on some of the kitchen cabinets. I suspected they were blood. Investigator Vaughn located a second clump of the victim's hair in the kitchen garbage can that was behind one of the cabinet doors that had blood on it.

The apartment showed no obvious signs of ransacking; however, the victim's wallet was missing. A white purse was located on a green upholstered chair in the victim's bedroom next to her bed. The purse was open but did not contain a wallet. The victim's vehicle was located in the garage that was beneath the rear of the building and was searched with negative results.

I consulted Investigator Jim Beikirch, our most senior crime scene specialist, about what the scene was telling us. A giant-sized man with a warm personality and quick wit, Investigator Beikirch was given the nickname "Bear" long before I got on the job. Our preliminary conclusions were identical.

It appeared the victim had prepared her meal, which consisted of a microwave dinner and a salad, in the kitchen and then began consuming it at the dining table in the living room area. Someone must have knocked on the victim's door while she was eating. By the position of the victim's slippers and her body, she must have got up from the table and answered the door since there was no sign of a forcible entry.

Based on where the victim's body lay and its condition, it appeared that her assailant forcibly knocked her to the floor, strangled her and then stabbed her with an unknown instrument that was not recovered at the scene. It appeared the perpetrator did a cursory search of the apartment subsequent to the attack but did not ransack it. The only item belonging to the victim that appeared to be missing at that time was her wallet.

After we inspected the crime scene, Investigator Vaughn and I interviewed the victim's neighbor about the circumstances of how she came to discover the murdered woman. We then drove to the Zone A Substation and met with the victim's son, who was a single, middle-aged man and employed as an administrator at one of the universities located in the Rochester area.

The victim's son said he ate dinner with his mother at least once a week in her apartment. When he was unable to get ahold of his mother to talk about having dinner the following evening, he contacted the neighbor and asked her to check on her. Having a key in her possession, the neighbor unlocked the victim's door once she did not answer it. Upon finding the unresponsive woman lying on the floor, she called 911.

The victim had no known enemies, according to her son. He described his mother as a gentle and friendly woman who still drove her own vehicle every day and lived her life to the fullest. The victim's neighbors confirmed his depiction of her. By all accounts, the victim was a personable and warmhearted woman who always had a nice a thing to say to everyone.

The responses of the victim's son did not raise our suspicion toward him during his interview. While I never removed anyone as a potential suspect, especially family and close friends, until the crime was solved, I qualified each individual based on the facts I had in front of me at the time of their interview.

To haphazardly accuse people of committing a serious crime against a loved one or family member without a hint of proof or suspicion just because statistics say they are the most likely suspects is stupid and screams incompetence. Such a method would not only cause undue emotional harm to someone who just suffered a huge personal loss, it certainly would alienate a potential ally that the police investigator may need in the future.

When a detective comes on too heavy, too fast and without merit, it only causes people who don't need a lawyer to ask for one. When that happens, the whole investigation starts to go south. The lawyers will dictate when, where and how the detective can ask questions, causing them to lose what little advantage they may have had. The only thing that could salvage the investigation at that point is the presence of physical evidence that connects a specific person to the crime scene, which is rare in the real world.

Investigator Vaughn and I agreed the victim's son appeared to be telling us the truth, and we had nothing to discredit his testimony at that point. None of the neighbors indicated that there was a problem between the victim and her only child. Our investigation was far from complete. If something came to light that put him back in our sights, we would reinterview him.

It was shortly after 1:00 a.m. the next day when Investigator Vaughn and I returned to the crime scene to locate the victim's bank and credit card numbers. We turned them over to a couple of detectives from the zone substations to follow up with the respective banks and credit card companies in order to determine if someone attempted to access those accounts or used the credit cards.

The Monroe County Medical Examiner's Office eventually arrived on the scene to conduct their preliminary investigation and remove the corpse. The autopsy, which would aid us in determining the cause and estimated time of death, would be conducted sometime later that morning. Investigator Beikirch said he would follow up with the medical examiner and let us know their findings.

If I had to guess, the victim met her tragic demise a few hours before her body was discovered and died as a result of strangulation. The multiple stab wounds were inflicted after the fact to make sure she was dead. This was a classic case of overkill. Either the killer was very angry with the victim or they wanted to make sure she would not miraculously regain consciousness to identify them as her assailant.

Investigator Vaughn and I left the crime scene for the second time and drove to the residence of *Tim Jacobs, one of the maintenance men employed at the apartment complex. It was brought to our attention that he was AWOL from work on the day of the murder and had not been heard from. We knocked on the front door of Jacobs' house, which was located on the east side of the city, and awakened his father.

Mr. Jacobs was pleasant for a man who had just been rousted out of bed at two in the morning. We kept it friendly as well and apologized for the intrusion. Mr. Jacobs advised that his son lived there with him but was not home. He suspected Tim was out getting high and drunk but claimed to not know his whereabouts. Based on our conversation, it sounded as though he was not happy with his son's choice of recreation and said it was affecting his work ethic. Mr. Jacobs was concerned about his son losing a job that he had held for more than ten years. We left a business card for Tim and asked his father to have him call us when he returned home.

After leaving the Jacobs residence, we drove to a twenty-four-hour gas station in the town of Penfield where the victim's credit card was used to purchase fuel on the evening she was murdered. According to the zone detectives, the card was used a couple hours after her body was discovered.

This potential lead went cold before we even knew it existed. Investigator Vaughn and I checked the surveillance tapes at the self-serve gas station but found the camera focused on the pump where the victim's credit card was used to pay for the fuel was not working. The night clerk on duty proved to be worthless, unable to offer us anything of value. Exhausted, with no workable leads to pursue, we called it a night at about four that morning.

After about four hours of sleep, I showered, got dressed and reported back to our headquarters office in downtown Rochester for a meeting. With the murder of an elderly woman, daily update meetings were going to be an unavoidable requirement of the investigation. Investigator Vaughn and I formulated an investigative plan just before we entered the conference room to discuss the case with our supervisors, including the chief deputy and major of operations. It was better to inform the higher-ups of what we were going to do than appear as though we needed direction.

Frustrated that we spent the morning discussing the case rather than working it, Investigator Vaughn and I drove out to Pittsford to commence our follow-up investigation. We decided to grab a quick sandwich in a sub

Image from the murder in Pittsford case. *Courtesy of Gene Renner.*

shop at Pittsford Plaza to put some fuel in our tired bodies. The plaza was one-fourth of a mile down the road from the apartment complex where the murder occurred.

Both of us had not eaten since the day before and were famished. We could tell our sugar levels must have been extremely low by the way we both felt and looked at the day ahead of us. Hunger and frustration was evolving into anger as our energy levels plummeted by the minute.

"I need to eat before we do anything," Investigator Vaughn exclaimed, as we pulled into the parking lot and made our way through the afternoon traffic over to the sub shop. It was tucked away in the east corner of the already bustling, large plaza. He was not a happy man.

"OK, Detective Cranky Pants," I responded.

"Aren't you hungry?" he asked, looking at me with a perplexed expression on his face.

"I'm beyond hungry. I'm Hangry," I said.

Laughing out loud, he asked, "Hangry? What the hell does that mean?"

"It's a combination of hunger and anger caused by the low sugar levels in our brain," I said, as he parked our unmarked police car between two other parked vehicles. My tone mimicked that of a physician explaining a medical condition to their patient.

As we walked from our police car to the restaurant, I noticed that the cool fall morning was blossoming into a beautiful sunny afternoon. September and October are my two favorite months of the year. They offer plenty of cool and crisp mornings that eventually give way to sapphire blue skies and pleasantly warm afternoons with minimal humidity. My mood improved by the time we ordered our food at the counter and sat down to await its arrival.

It is amazing how a fulfilling meal can change one's countenance. Despite the lack of sleep, I was ready to go another twelve hours. After we devoured our submarine sandwiches and bowls of soup while mulling over the case, including the missing maintenance man, Investigator Vaughn and I drove to the apartment complex and went to the main office, where we met with the superintendent.

After obtaining the work schedules and contact information of each the employees, we asked him if we could meet with the maintenance crew who were on duty. The superintendent agreed to our request; however, he offered that he did not suspect any of his employees of committing this crime. He said all of them adored the victim because she always treated them so kindly when they serviced her apartment. We assured him that no one was being targeted as a suspect, but we needed to speak with anyone who might have had contact with the victim over the past few days.

With his assistance, the three maintenance men were summoned to their shop, which was located in a building behind one of the apartment buildings in the rear of the complex. Much to our pleasant surprise, Tim Jacobs had reported to work that morning. The two other workers were Hispanic men with friendly dispositions. Jacobs was polite and friendly as well and apologized for not being at home when we called on him earlier.

All three men exhibited remorse for the victim and identified her as one of the nicest residents in the complex. They said she even went out of her way to give all of them money gifts at Christmas time. I asked the men to voluntarily follow us in their maintenance truck to the Monroe County Sheriff's Zone A Substation to be interviewed and submit fingerprints and saliva samples for comparison purposes. I also asked that they voluntarily consent to a search of their personal vehicles. All three men agreed to our requests and followed Investigator Vaughn and me over to the substation.

Tim Jacobs said his father had driven him to work that morning, so his vehicle was not at the apartment complex. He agreed to take us to it after we completed our business at the substation. The vehicles of the other two maintenance men were at the apartment complex and would be searched by Investigator Beikirch after he retrieved their saliva samples and fingerprints. We would make separate arrangements for Jacobs's vehicle when we located it.

It was shortly after 1:00 p.m. when we arrived at the substation and commenced the interviews. Investigator Vaughn and I interviewed the two Hispanic maintenance men first, leaving Jacobs's interview for last since we had to assist him with locating his vehicle. Both men provided us with solid alibis as to their whereabouts the day and evening of the murder.

One of the men disclosed that Tim Jacobs had a drug addiction to crack cocaine and would disappear from work now and then to get high. Both men confirmed Jacobs had skipped out of work in the afternoon the day of the murder and did not return during their work shift. Neither man knew if Jacobs returned to the complex that evening. After both men were interviewed, we turned them over to Investigator Beikirch for fingerprints, DNA samples and consensual searches of their personal vehicles back at the apartment complex.

Investigator Vaughn and I met with Tim Jacobs in the interview room sometime around 1:40 p.m. For a guy who was supposedly hooked on crack, Jacobs sported a thick and paunchy build at five feet, ten inches tall. He had a ruddy, freckled complexion and friendly face. He was soft-spoken when he talked.

Just in case things turned adversarial during the interview, we had him give his fingerprints and DNA sample while he was waiting to be interviewed. He appeared nervous, but it could have been because he knew we were aware of his crack habit as a result of our discussions with his father and two co-workers, who were actually his subordinates.

Jacobs advised that he had been employed by the company that owned the apartment complex for twelve and a half years and currently held the position of assistant manager. This role required him to have personal contact with the residents while fielding complaints and addressing issues within the complex.

Jacobs was quick to tell us that he did not know anything about the murder nor did he suspect anyone. He also offered that he last saw the victim on the morning of the day she was found murdered. Jacobs said she was driving her vehicle out of the complex while he was painting the exterior of one of the buildings near to her apartment. He said it was around 9:30 a.m.

Jacobs admitted that he was addicted to crack cocaine and confirmed he left work early without permission from his boss to get high. He offered the following account of his afternoon and evening: Jacobs said he left work at 1:30 p.m. and drove his maroon two-door Oldsmobile Alero to the area of Parsells Avenue and Denver Street in Rochester to buy crack cocaine from a black male dealer he knew only as "Danny" and purchased fifteen dollars' worth of crack.

Jacobs said he then drove to Ellison Park, which is in the town of Brighton, and smoked his crack cocaine while he sat in his vehicle. He remained in Ellison Park from 2:30 until about 3:00 p.m. He then drove home and remained there from 3:30 p.m. until 4:30 p.m. Jacobs said he spoke with his father briefly while he was home.

Jacobs said he drove around the city for about forty-five minutes and ended up back in the area of Parcells Avenue and Denver Street, where he traded the use of his vehicle for ten dime bags of crack cocaine with Danny the crack dealer. This is a frequent practice among crack addicts and their illicit pharmacists on the street, commonly referred to as "car rental by crackhead."

Sitting fat with ten dime bags of crack to suck through his pipe, Jacobs said he walked around the Main Street and North Winton Avenue area of the city while he got high. Jacobs said he stopped by a neighborhood saloon known as the Main Place, located on the east end of Main Street, and visited with a male friend for a short time. He identified the friend as *Ken Marcher. Jacobs said he continued to walk around the same area until about 3:00 a.m. after he left the bar.

Jacobs said he first heard about the murder when he called his father around 3:15 a.m. His father further advised him about the two sheriff's detectives who stopped by to talk to him. Jacobs said he immediately walked home after hearing this news and arrived there sometime between 3:30 a.m. and 3:45 a.m. Jacobs said his father gave him our business cards upon his arrival. He called Investigator Vaughn's cellphone and left him a message.

Jacobs said it wasn't until he viewed the early news that morning that he found out the identity of the murder victim. His father had told him that a person was murdered at the complex but hadn't told him who. Jacobs said his father drove him to work since his car was still in the possession of the crack dealer. Jacobs said he called and left messages for both Investigator Vaughn and me after he arrived at work that morning. We were able to confirm this after listening to our phone messages.

The jury was still out on this guy. He appeared to have provided us with a reasonable explanation of his whereabouts on the day and evening in question. He called us as soon as he learned we were looking for him. He disclosed his crack addiction and drug abuse activity. And he appeared to relax after telling us his story. However, we still needed to take a look at his vehicle before we decided what to do next.

We did not become adversarial with Jacobs and only requested a specific timeline of his whereabouts and activity on the day and evening of the murder. We had nothing to challenge Jacobs with other than him being a crackhead. We wanted to avoid having to apply for a search warrant to search his vehicle. We did not have enough probable cause to obtain one, so it was imperative that we did not give Jacobs the impression we were judging him in a negative light for being a crackhead and keep him cooperative. Gaining Jacobs's voluntary consent to search his vehicle would save us a lot of hassle and heartache. But first we had to locate Danny the crack dealer.

Jacobs sat in the back of our unmarked police car unhandcuffed as we drove him into the city to find his Oldsmobile Alero. He directed us to a house on the corner of Grand Avenue and Denver Street. His crack dealer's crib was the first-floor apartment located in the rear of the multiple dwelling. We did not see any sign of Danny or Jacobs's vehicle, so we parked down Denver Street and waited for either one to show up.

We did not have to wait long. Within ten minutes of setting up we observed Jacobs's Oldsmobile being driven down Denver Street toward Parsells Avenue. Two black males were in the vehicle; neither of them was Danny. I asked Jacobs if he gave anyone else permission to use his vehicle. He responded, "No." I asked him if he knew either of the males in the car. He said, "No."

I asked Jacobs if he wanted us to stop the car and find out what was going on. He agreed. I then pulled up behind the vehicle as it was stopped at the corner of Denver Street and Parsells Avenue. Investigator Vaughn and I stepped out of our car, walked up to Jacobs's vehicle and directed the driver to pull over to the side of the road after he made the turn onto Parsells Avenue. He complied without incident.

Both the driver and the passenger stepped out of Jacobs's Alero without a fuss. Our approach was low-key and friendly as we carefully patted them down for weapons. We maintained officer safety without making them our enemies to cultivate cooperation. Good street cops do this numerous times every day. Major Crimes detectives don't usually do the stop-and-frisk routine nearly as much, but it is good practice to keep up on one's skills.

Once the pat downs were completed, both subjects agreed to talk with us while we stood on the sidewalk. Jacobs chose to remain in the back seat of our vehicle while we conducted the interviews. I got the feeling he was trying to stay out of sight. The nineteen-year-old driver identified himself as *Demetrius Moss. His eighteen-year-old passenger identified himself as *Louis Perez. Of course, neither of them was in possession of any identification, including a legal driver's license. As was the custom in dealing with street urchins and mopes, both were identified via their local criminal records. Both had been convicted of misdemeanor-level drug possession.

After their identities were confirmed, we talked to them about how they came into possession of the vehicle. I paired up with Demetrius and Investigator Vaughn paired up with Louis. It had shaped up to be a semiwarm afternoon, so I led Demetrius to the shade of a tree just off the sidewalk to escape the heat of the sun. A slight breeze made the location a perfect place for conducting an impromptu interview. I took my time as I quizzed Demetrius about the "who, what, where, when and how."

Both subjects offered the exact same account. They stated *Danny Johnson, aka Danny the crack dealer, loaned them Jacobs's vehicle later in the evening the night before. Both subjects were familiar with Tim Jacobs and said he frequented the area to buy crack and knew the car they were in possession of belonged to him. They also identified him to be the person slumping down in the backseat of our vehicle. It was obvious Jacobs did not want to be seen by the citizens parading by to take in the afternoon matinee of the police shaking down a couple of local hoods.

Both young men refused to provide us with their dope dealing friend's cellphone number or confirm he was slinging crack. At my request,

Demetrius called Danny from his own cellphone. When Danny answered, Demetrius filled him in. "Five-O needs to ax you some questions 'bout that geeker's ride."

He then handed me his cellphone. I tried to keep the device from touching my ear as I held it up to my head and stepped away from Demetrius. Investigator Vaughn was still speaking with Louis several feet away. Danny was cagey but agreed to speak with me when I told him we were investigating the murder of an elderly woman and not his activities. I purposely did not advise him of when or where the crime occurred.

He confirmed that Jacobs let him use his car for a "fee" but would not admit to selling him crack or admit the fee consisted of crack cocaine. When I asked Danny what time he took possession of Jacobs's vehicle, he said it was sometime in the late evening, around 10:00 p.m., a clear contradiction of what Jacobs told us earlier that afternoon during his interview at the substation. Promising that I would not shake him down and arrest him for dealing, I asked Danny to respond to our location so we could talk to him further. He hesitantly agreed after I reminded him that we were more concerned about solving the vicious murder of an elderly woman.

We could put Danny's lawbreaking transgressions off for another day. We'd get the narco squad on him eventually. Lock him up for selling to an undercover cop and we'd own him. If he had anything to do with this murder, then we'd be in a better position to press him for the truth. It was too soon to put him in or out of this thing. So I chose to keep him cooperative with his fate in limbo.

All I knew at that point was Jacobs may have lied to us if we chose to believe his drug rep. Until I can corroborate someone's account with either physical evidence or other credible testimony, I don't place much weight on it.

I returned Demetrius's cellphone to him and told him to stick around. I returned to our vehicle and retrieved a consent-to-search form from my briefcase in the trunk. I then sat in the driver's seat, rolled up the windows and blasted the air conditioning to keep Tim Jacobs and me comfortable as we spoke.

I asked him if we could search his vehicle. I chose not to share what Danny Johnson told me. My mission at that moment in time was to search Jacobs's vehicle with his consent, not challenge him about his truthfulness. That would come later.

Jacobs gave me, and any other officers I designated, verbal consent to search his vehicle. At my request, he signed the waiver form I had filled out while speaking with him to memorialize his consent. By law, verbal consent is sufficient in New York State; however, having the person's signature on a consent-to-search form, or a recording of the verbal consent, makes for an easier suppression hearing. Undoubtedly, the person's lawyer is going to file motions that the police lied about obtaining their client's voluntary consent to search, and/or it was coerced.

A few minutes later, Investigator Vaughn signaled me to come over to Jacobs's vehicle, which was still parked in the street along the curb in front of our vehicle. He directed my attention to the floor behind the front passenger seat as I approached the vehicle. I peered inside and observed a health insurance identification card bearing the victim's name lying on the floor next to a broken decorative ceramic bowl.

We pulled Demetrius aside and asked him about the identification card. He offered that he had observed the card along with other items in the vehicle that he described as personal papers and a woman's wallet that appeared to belong to an elderly woman. He said the wallet fell out of the vehicle when he first took possession of it the night before. He thought the car most likely belonged to Jacobs's grandmother, so he threw them into the back seat.

"Them things aren't there now," Demetrius advised us.

"Where are they?" Investigator Vaughn asked.

"Don't know," he replied. "One of my homegirls saw the dude rifling through his car earlier this morning." Demetrius motioned his head toward our vehicle when he said, "dude." He was obviously referring to Tim Jacobs.

"How early you talking?" I asked

"I don't know. It was still dark out," he said.

"Where'd this happen?" Investigator Vaughn asked.

"Outside my crib," he informed us.

"Where were you?" I asked.

"Sleeping. I parked the car right in front of my place."

Demetrius provided us with the name and physical description of the young woman who observed Jacobs going through his vehicle. He then pointed out her house. Investigator Vaughn observed her arrive home several minutes later. We walked across the street and spoke with the young woman. She confirmed what Demetrius had told us and agreed to give us a statement.

I notified Lieutenant Schirtz and advised him what we had found thus far. I requested crime scene technicians to respond and process Jacobs's vehicle. I also asked for another team to respond to our location to take statements from our growing list of witnesses. We needed to get Jacobs out of the area before the technicians showed up to hook his car back to our secured facility to search it.

Danny showed up just as Investigators Tom Passmore and Kevin Garvey arrived on scene to take statements. I thanked Danny for following through and turned him over to Passmore and Garvey. I also introduced them to the other witnesses and provided a synopsis of their testimony.

It was about 4:25 p.m. when Investigator Vaughn and I pulled away from the curb with Jacobs still sitting in the back seat. We headed to our downtown office to discuss the issues at hand with our less-than-honest maintenance man. As we were driving to the office, I asked Jacobs what he thought should happen to the person who murdered the elderly woman who had treated him so kindly.

"They should be dealt with according to the law," he responded.

Once we arrived at our building fifteen minutes later, Jacobs called his father from his cellphone to let him know where he was and that he would be home later. We still had not told him what we found inside his vehicle. After Jacobs hung up with his father, we took the elevator up to the second floor and walked into the Criminal Investigations Section office. He was not handcuffed and walking about freely.

Our office was located in the old city hall building in the heart of downtown Rochester on the corner of Broad Street and North Fitzhugh Street, across from the Watts Building, home to the Monroe County District Attorney's Office. Our headquarters in the Monroe County Public Safety Building was being renovated. Ironically, the Criminal Investigations Section was located in a building that housed mostly private law firms, many of whom had criminal defense lawyers on staff.

Jacobs was escorted to the area that housed the Major Crimes Unit and directed to take a seat in Investigator Vaughn's office. The office was small with old-fashioned tall windows along two walls. Jacobs sat in a chair between the two desks. Investigator Vaughn sat at his desk, while I sat at Investigator Paul Siena's desk. We rolled our chairs away from around the desks to be closer to Jacobs. I don't like having a physical barrier between the suspect I am interviewing and me.

Jacobs had developed into a full-fledged suspect. He did not know it yet, but it was just a matter of time before we confronted him about the lie and the victim's items we found in his vehicle. Thinking ahead, I decided to read him his rights before we got started rather than having to stop the interview when we were in the midst of confronting him.

I told Jacobs that he was not under arrest or in custody; however, because he was seated in our office, I thought it appropriate we read him his Miranda warnings. He seemed OK with the suggestion and didn't ask any questions about being a suspect, so I pulled out my yellow rights waiver card from my wallet and advised him of his rights by reading them verbatim from the card. After listening carefully, he waived them and agreed to keep speaking with us.

I then commenced a monologue expressing our appreciation for his cooperation that afternoon and his honesty about his crack addiction. That being said, I told Jacobs that his account of his whereabouts the night of the murder was starting to unravel. I then advised Jacobs that Danny and his two associates offered us a remarkably different account than the one he provided us.

Investigator Vaughn remained silent, so I continued. In two-man interviews, usually one detective takes the lead and the other picks up the slack when the lead interviewer runs out of words and questions. I told Jacobs how Danny said he loaned him the car at about 10:00 p.m., not 5:30 as he told us. I told Jacobs how Demetrius told us about the elderly woman's wallet that he observed on the back seat of his car. I then told Jacobs about the female who watched him rifling through his vehicle earlier that morning as she was leaving for work.

I paused for a moment to let it all resonate in Jacobs's mind, allowing Investigator Vaughn the opportunity to chime in. He remained silent, looking at Jacobs, who had been looking down at the floor the whole time I was speaking. I kept going, pointing out to Jacobs that he did not share these events with us when we spoke at the substation earlier that afternoon. I then dropped the bomb on him. I informed Jacobs that we found the victim's health insurance card in his vehicle.

Sounding very surprised, Jacobs looked up at me for the first time and said, "You found her health insurance card?" His response came across as, "Oh, no! I thought I cleaned everything out. How could I have left that in there."

"Yes we did," I said. "You must have accidentally left it behind when you were cleaning your car out this morning." He gave me no response, so I continued.

"We believe you made a tragic mistake last night and killed Rose." I paused for a moment. "We believe your crack addiction is to blame." Jacobs was staring at the carpeted floor in silence. Investigator Vaughn remained quiet.

I continued, "Tim, you need to start telling us the truth about what really happened last night. I don't think you meant for it to happen, but no one's going to know unless you tell us. Rose isn't here to tell us. Either you really hated that old woman and meant to do her harm, or you went there with no intention to hurt her and just snapped because of what the crack is doing to your mind.

"But only you can tell us. Her family and friends have a right to know how such a tragedy could have occurred, Tim. If you don't share your side of the situation, then everyone will have no choice but to think of you as nothing more than a brutal and evil murderer. And I know that's not the case. But you have to speak up and tell us what happened."

Still looking at the floor, Jacobs began to shake his head back and forth. "I don't like where this is going," he said. "My dad told me that I should get a lawyer and not say anything if you guys think I did this."

"That's your decision to make, Tim. Not your father's. We just want to know what happened because, as I said before, Rose isn't here to tell us her side."

Right on cue, Investigator Vaughn said in a reassuring voice, "We think you're a good guy, Tim. The public wants to forgive people who make mistakes. This was a terrible mistake."

We did not view the comment about his dad telling him to get a lawyer as an invocation or request for a lawyer. I considered it open contemplation. I then told Jacobs that his dad was already broken up about his crack addiction and cried about it last night when we spoke to him. "It's time to take responsibility for your actions, Tim," I said.

Investigator Vaughn said, "This was a tragedy of circumstances, but you will be viewed as a coldhearted killer unless you tell us your side." Many people who commit heinous crimes have a deep desire to explain why and how it came to occur so others won't think they are as evil as their vicious acts. We were utilizing this strategy since Jacobs did not possess a violent history or a criminal background.

We continued to maintain a soft and supportive tone with him. While we asserted our belief that he committed this horrible crime, we never raised our voices or became hostile with him. We continued to displace the blame away from him. I told Jacobs that if he chose to not share his side of the situation, then his father and family would most likely have to live with the stigma of spawning and raising a vicious, coldhearted killer. I suggested that this would not be the case if he shared what happened and took responsibility for his actions.

"The public would understand that this horrible outcome was the result of you being a crack addict. Everyone would know that crack cocaine is the real evil entity this case," I said, displacing blame from him onto the drug. "Your twelve years of excellent service at the apartment complex serves as a testimonial to what you are really about, Tim. You telling the truth would let others know just how terrible this drug truly is…to make such a good and caring person do such a tragic thing."

Investigator Vaughn said, "It's like breaking up with a close girlfriend, Tim. It's something no one wants to do, but after you take the first step and just do it, you'll feel better afterward."

Jacobs continued to stare at the floor, appearing to give what we were saying some serious thought. However, I was concerned that he might be thinking about asking for a lawyer, so I changed the subject rather than move in for the close. I didn't think he was quite there yet. We could always come back to it after some more rapport building.

"You hungry?" I asked him.

"I'm getting there," he answered with a smile, lifting his head up and looking at me. "Look at me. I'm an overweight crack addict. I still like to eat." The three of us shared a laugh.

We decided on Bill Grays, a popular local burger establishment, and ordered cheeseburgers and fries. After placing the order for takeout and making arrangements to have it delivered, Jacobs asked us a question out of the blue. "What would happen to me if I admitted to this?" he asked.

The strategy had worked. After you do enough interviews and interrogations, you get a feel when to press and when to let up. Letting up on this guy turned out to be the right thing to do. I sensed that he trusted us more. He went from total denial to thinking about it.

Investigator Vaughn answered Jacobs's question. "You'd be arrested and arraigned in town court tonight." There was no way to sugarcoat the murder of an elderly woman.

"What then?" Jacobs asked.

"The judge has the option to set bail or put you in jail with no bail," I answered.

"Is drug treatment an option?" he asked.

I said, "No. This is too serious for a drug treatment option."

Jacobs nodded his head up and down. "I understand."

We wanted to be honest with him. Murderers go to prison for a long time, especially those who kill a defenseless elderly woman.

Still pondering his next move, Jacobs asked, "What would I be charged with?"

"Depends on what you tell us happened and your culpable mental state at the time," I said. There was some truth to the statement but not much. Unless he could prove this was in self-defense, which was ludicrous, he was going to be charged with murder in the first degree. I did not want to deter our suspect from telling us what happened; therefore, I left him with some hope that he might be able to explain his way out of this.

Again, I reminded Jacobs that he would be viewed as a vicious killer unless he provided us with his side. I told him to not let the drug dealers look like the heroes in this case because of their testimony against him. I told him to deny them the undeserved limelight and adulation and tell us what happened with Rose. I told him that I held them partly responsible for this horrible event since they aided him in becoming a crack addict.

Investigator Vaughn said, "Tim, you're a good guy. Who do you care about?"

"My father," Jacobs answered.

"It would be better for your father to hear what happened from you first than the media," I said. "Tell us what happened, and we'll make sure we tell your dad before this goes public."

"Tim, this is not your fault," Investigator Vaughn said. "The public wants to forgive." Displacing the blame seemed to be working with this suspect.

Jacobs held his face in his hands as he sat silent for about minute. We remained silent since he appeared to be in deep thought. I had a feeling this was it, and I believe Investigator Vaughn was feeling the same. So we sat in silence there for another minute until Jacobs finally spoke.

"Get ready to write this down," he said softly.

"Write what down?" I asked him.

"I'm gonna tell you what happened last night," Jacobs said.

Tim Jacobs said everything he told us about how he spent the afternoon of the day the victim was found dead in her apartment was accurate except for the actual time he traded his car for crack with Danny Johnson. Jacobs confirmed that Johnson's version was accurate; the dope transaction for the use of his vehicle occurred later at night. Jacobs said he returned to the apartment complex sometime around six thirty the night the victim was discovered dead.

Sitting on his chair and looking straight ahead at the file cabinets in front of him, Jacobs said he had been borrowing money from the victim over the past few months and using it to buy crack cocaine. Making a decision to ask her for more money, Jacobs said he drove back to the complex and parked his vehicle behind the victim's building. He entered it through the rear entrance and walked up to the victim's apartment door. As he was knocking on the door, Jacobs said he remembered that he still owed her money from past loans.

When the victim opened the door partially, Jacobs said he forcibly pushed it open. The force caused the victim to fall back onto the floor, landing on her back. When she began to yell for help, he jumped on top of her with his entire body. He forced one hand over her mouth and wrapped his meaty arm around her fragile neck and squeezed. Her writhing body went limp within seconds.

Jacobs said he then looked around the victim's apartment for money and grabbed her wallet from the white purse that was on the chair in her bedroom. When he returned to where the victim was lying, he noticed she was moving so he placed his hand over her mouth and strangled her for a second time. To make sure she was dead, he grabbed a pair of large scissors that had fallen off the nearby ironing board during the initial attack and stabbed her about the chest and neck repeatedly.

Jacobs leaned back in his chair, looked at the ceiling for a moment and continued to talk as Investigator Vaughn and I listened without interrupting him. We'd save the questions for later. We wanted him to keep talking.

"I grabbed the scissors and wallet and left," he said. "I tossed the scissors out my car window when I drove up the I-590 ramp from Monroe Ave. I used the money from her wallet to buy more crack. I used her American Express Card to buy gas at a Mobil station on Empire Boulevard."

"How much cash was in her wallet?" Investigator Vaughn asked.

"$110," he said.

"Where did you dump the wallet after you retrieved it from your car this morning?" I asked.

Jacobs answered, "Grand Avenue and Culver Road."

I asked, "Will you help us look for the wallet and scissors?"

"Yes," he said. "I never went there intending to kill her. I just snapped."

Like I've witnessed so many times before, Jacobs's whole posture changed once he told us his story. He appeared relaxed. He wasn't leaning forward with his face in his hands or staring out into empty space. He was more engaging as we continued to ask him questions for specific details while Investigator Vaughn commenced typing Jacobs's written statement. Without solicitation, Jacobs looked directly at me and said, "You were right. I feel better now that I got it off my chest."

Jacobs had admitted to the murder at about 6:10 p.m. We took a break to eat our cheeseburgers and fries at about 6:35 p.m. Jacobs ate all his food and continued to answer our questions more candidly than before his confession.

At our request, Jacobs read his three-page written statement aloud and made several corrections and placed his initials next to each one. The mistakes were made intentionally to illustrate that Jacobs read his statement and understood it. Having him read it aloud proved that he could, in fact, read.

When Jacobs was finished reading the statement, Investigator Vaughn asked, "Do you want to make any more changes?"

"No," Jacobs answered.

"Does your statement accurately reflect what we talked about and what you told us?" I asked.

"Yes."

"Is it the truth?" I asked.

"Yes," Jacobs answered.

At my request, Jacobs affixed his signature on his written statement. He then handed me his personal keys to the apartment complex. He also provided us written consent to search his home for additional evidence and accompanied Investigator Vaughn and I to the areas he ditched the victim's scissors and the wallet. He assisted us with the search, but neither item was located.

After we handed off Jacobs to a Road Patrol deputy for his arraignment in Pittsford Town Court, where he was charged with murder in the first degree, Investigator Vaughn and I drove back to Jacobs's residence to recover the clothes he was wearing when he committed the murder. It was shortly after 10:30 p.m. when we located his clothes in his bedroom.

We also took the opportunity to sit down with Jacobs's father and advise him of his son's wicked act and arrest. The news visibly shook him, erasing all suspicion that he possessed any knowledge of the killing or assisted his son after the fact. Not wanting to leave the already frail and unhealthy man alone after hitting him with such a devastating notification, we had Mr. Jacobs call his son and daughter-in-law to come over and sit with him for a while. We left shortly after they arrived.

After we received word that Jacobs had been held without bail and notified the victim's son of the arrest, Investigator Vaughn and I stopped at Jeremiah's Tavern on our way home for some Buffalo wings and decompress time. We had closed a murder case approximately twenty-four hours after being called in to investigate the crime. We did what was expected of us. For a brief moment, we could relish this feeling of accomplishment. The paper work, court preparation and testifying would come another day.

# EPILOGUE

Tim Jacobs's father used a large chunk of his retirement annuity money to hire a high-priced lawyer to defend his son. Initially, I felt bad for the guy. He was pissing his money away on a worthless cause. I was disgusted with his son for not utilizing the free services of a competent public defender instead of draining his father of his hard-earned money to defend him for a crime that he admitted to committing. That is until I listened to a few of their phone conversations that were recorded at the jail.

All inmate phone calls from the Monroe County Jail are recorded with the knowledge of the inmate and the person they are talking to. A recorded notification that the call is being recorded is played for them at the beginning of each phone call. Yet, incredibly, we still hear many inmates who are awaiting trial make unintended admissions and other incriminating statements during those phone conversations. Almost always, these recorded statements will be passed along to the prosecutors and used against the inmates at their trials.

Tim Jacobs did not make that mistake; however, both he and his father made some not-so-flattering comments about me during several of their conversations. For whatever reason, I ended up doing the lion's share of testifying in the court proceedings. Investigator Vaughn intercepted several recorded conversations between Jacobs and his father talking about my testifying at the suppression hearing and trial.

Both men were overheard referring to me as a "dirty cop." Jacobs's father said I should win an Academy Award for lying so well when I testified in the court proceedings. He assured his son that the high-priced lawyer would get even with me. "Don't worry, Honey. Joe will get him. Joe will get him," he said confidently. I found it incredible and sickening that this father was referring to his nearly thirty-year-old son who murdered a defenseless old woman as "Honey." True to form, Investigator Vaughn recorded these conversations onto a CD and presented it to me as a gift to be played at my retirement party. I didn't have a party when I retired.

While Jacobs's lawyer did a commendable job with his cross-examination, he never accused me of lying or any other unlawful or unethical conduct. He knew we had his client six ways to Sunday with no wiggle room, fair and square. We had a full, legally obtained confession from his client that corroborated the crime scene, witness testimony that contradicted his attempted alibi and the victim's blood on his clothing. The trial ended with Jacobs being convicted of murder in the first degree and a life sentence in the custody of the New York State Department of Corrections. Case closed.

# Final Comments

If you are in law enforcement or aspire to work in the field, it is my sincere hope that this book has inspired you to do your best each and every day you wear the badge. Thank you for taking the time to read it.

While I consider some of the cases I worked, including the ones shared in this book, to be memorable moments in my career, I don't view these experiences to be more remarkable than those of other police officers. Every cop could write a book about their personal experiences while on the job and share a story worth telling. I have a few more experiences of my own left to tell and many more from several of my esteemed colleagues. We'll see what the future holds.

If I never write again, then I leave you with this final thought: the police investigator works for God and God alone. Their sole purpose is to pursue and expose the truth. Only after that mission is completed do you pursue and confront the perpetrators and enforce the law. Don't get caught up in the emotional aspect of the crimes you're investigating or the political pressures surrounding high-profile cases. Set your pride aside and don't confuse your job with prosecuting and dispensing justice. That responsibility is left to the prosecutor, jury and judge.

Pride has clouded my judgment at times and alienated those close to me. Treat it like your enemy, for it will not only alienate your colleagues but also the suspects, victims and witnesses you come into contact with. Work from a foundation of humility and meekness. It will manifest into inner strength and restraint.

Sometimes the truth doesn't always wind up being what everyone anticipated. If a police detective is not totally dedicated to finding the truth, first and foremost, they will eventually fail when it counts the most. Sometimes the truth is too elusive to be found when we most desire it. However, every case—no matter how cold or complicated—is just one phone call away from being solved. Never lose sight of that.

# About the Author

Retired investigator sergeant Patrick Crough served thirty years with the Monroe County Sheriff's Office as a college intern and police officer. After serving in the Marine Unit and on the Road Patrol, he worked assignments in the Violent Warrant Squad and the Vice and Narcotics Unit as an undercover officer.

After being promoted to the rank of investigator, he was assigned to the Major Crimes Unit, where he investigated some of the most heinous crimes committed in the Greater Rochester area for over two decades. He also served as a hostage negotiator on the Monroe County Sheriff's Hostage Rescue Team during the same time period.

In May 2009, Patrick Crough authored and published *The Serpents among Us: How to Protect Your Children from Sexual Predators; A Police Investigator's Perspective.* The book was written to educate parents about the manipulative techniques child predators utilize to gain access to a child they are targeting.

When Patrick Crough retired from the Monroe County Sheriff's Office in April 2010, he held the rank of investigator sergeant, in charge of the Major Crimes Unit and commander of the Hostage Rescue Team. He currently teaches basic and advanced interrogation techniques to other sworn police officers and detectives around the country for BowMac Educational Services/ Law Enforcement Consultants and serves as president of Millstone Justice Children's Advocacy Organization, a nonprofit corporation that is dedicated to teaching parents how to keep their children safe from child predators. For more information, please visit the website MillstoneJustice.org.

Visit us at
www.historypress.net